Index

15 Great Quilts with Batiks and 'Bali Pop' 2½" Strips

Basic instructions are on pages 80, 44 - 47

Painting hot wax with a piece of sponge

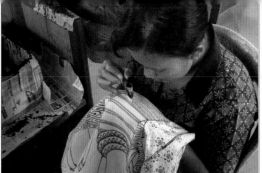

Applying fine lines and dots of hot wax

Stamping hot wax on white fabric

Batiks

Balinese culture and design are continuously linked with an intricate heritage enchanted by the charm and fascination of Batik fabric.

Traditional Batik fabrics are painstakingly decorated by hand with ethnic patterns, hot wax and colorful dyes.

Once you actually see Batik fabric being stamped and dyed by hand, it is hard to want to sew or quilt with any other fabric. Batik work requires a fabric of superior quality and tight weave in order to hold the hot wax.

Hand applied stamps and colors add intrinsic value to every inch of cloth.

Leafing through dozens of Batik patterns

The Best Moments

The best moments on the trip I took to Bali weren't the bath I took with an elephant, inclusion in celebrations on the beach, or absorption into the culture and beliefs. Terrific experiences to be sure, but they didn't inspire me as much as a visit to a Batik factory.

Bingo! This is why I came to Bali. What better souvenir than fabric I stamped and dyed myself?

The "factory" I visited was like a large backyard that involved the entire family and a few neighbors.

Stamped Batik

I stamped hot beeswax on yards of fabric in a shed letting the fabric fall on a clean floor. Choosing from dozens of intricate design stamps made of copper (called caps) — fish, butterflies, circles, geckos, flowers, leaves, swirls and more — was fun.

The fabric was dipped and scrunched with colorful dyes and powders on plastic tarps.

To remove the wax, the fabric was put in an oil drum filled with boiling water (heated by a wood fire) and stirred with a big stick. Finally I hung my fabric on little nails on drying racks in the sun. It all seemed to work like clockwork... yards of beautiful colored fabric and done with my own hands.

Needless to say my fabric was just a sampler. Skilled workers made fabrics with multiple dye baths, a variety of colors, and series of stamped designs plus swirled and mottled colors that only an expert can accomplish.

After a day spent making yards of beautiful fabric, I made a trip to the batik store to purchase more fabric — more colors, more designs, more variations. It is hard to choose, as each one seems more beautiful than the last.

Bunching fabric for dyeing and drying

Running fabric through a vat of dye

Soaking fabric to remove excess color

Intricate copper stamps (called caps)

Repetitive patterns are stamped one at a time.

Applying hot wax to fabric yardage

Tulis Batik

I also tried another type of Batik fabric called Tulis Batik. With this technique every line or dot is drawn individually with a hot wax tool that has a small spout on the end (called a canting).

Needless to say, this original way of doing Batik — before copper stamps were developed — is extremely time intensive. An artist can literally spend months applying wax to a length of cloth. And some fabrics and sarongs require more than one layer of wax and dye.

For this method, my simple drawings of little elephants, flowers, women and fish were traced onto fabric with the special drawing tool for hot wax. I had to be careful to connect all the lines. Then a sponge was used to apply dye colors to individual areas.

Again the fabric was boiled to remove the wax. These small designs were made into decorative panels - ready to surround with Batiks for one-of-a-kind quilts.

Sampler Batik panels like these are available as small pieces and greeting cards.

Boiling fabric to remove wax

Traditional Fabrics

In Bali great importance is attached to textiles and their making. The word "Batik" is Indonesian in origin and has been done in Indonesia for over 300 years.

The ancient Batik process is truly fascinating. Once observed or experienced it instills a full appreciation for the many steps and processes involved in producing a single yard of fabric.

The completely hand-done nature of the process with its uniqueness and one-of-a-kind nature develops that human connection between the creators and users.

Gorgeous fabric is perfect for anyone who appreciates handwork.

Ikat Fabrics

Another common handwoven textile is Ikat. It is made by tieing and dyeing the threads in a design before weaving. Amazing little people, chickens, animals and geometric patterns are created.

Songket Fabric

Special handwoven Songket cloth is woven on traditional hand-operated looms. The cloth contains complex, decorative motifs woven in gold and silver threads to create a rich brocade textile.

Batik Fabrics

Constantly inspired by memories and visions of Bali, I love collecting the variety of colors, hues, shades and patterns that are available in magical Batik fabrics.

Every time I look at these quilts, I am reminded of the beautiful and colorful island. The memories of friendly people overflow in my heart, mind and soul. I see the colors and feel the special blessings of Bali again and again.

The front of a Batik fabrics store reflects the treasures that are inside.

Hanging my Batik fabric out to dry

Colorful completed Batiks dry in the sun.

KS...Inspired by Bali

The sun on the horizon

Morning at the beach

Colorful sunrise

Jukung typical outrigger

Visit the ocean day

Pura Tanah Lot temple

Sunrise

pieced by Donna Perrotta
quilted by Sue Needle

Rediscover the blessing of a sunrise. Stunning colors combine in a diamond pattern to make this quilt colorful.

Be thankful and bless the dawning of each day with this especially beautiful quilt. You'll discover a special heritage and meaning along the way.

instructions on pages 24 - 27

FABRIC USED: Strawberry Fields
"Bali Pop" by *Hoffman*

Lush greens in the forest

Forest monkeys

Villagers visit the forest

Carved stone monkeys

Long tailed macaque

Emerald Forest

pieced by Rose Ann Pegram
quilted by Susan Corbett

Trees, vines and clear blue skies make their way into the colors of this earthy quilt to create an enduring palette for a warm inviting quilt.

Bali is an especially inspiring and magical place. Bali – colorful, glamorous, decorated everywhere and friendly makes it one of the world's most celebrated destinations.

instructions on pages 28 - 29

FABRIC USED: Mint Chip "Bali Pop" by *Hoffman*

Painted trash truck

Intricate bloom

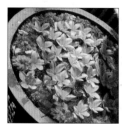

Blessings bowl

Colorful ginger bloom

Striking orchids

Water lilies in bloom

Lotus blossoms

Water lilies in the morning

Lotus flowers and pods

Beautiful pink flowers

Bright ginger blooms

Bowl of blessings and water

Sunshine Garden

pieced by Rose Ann Pegram
quilted by Susan Corbett

Fabric colors literally glow with the vibrancy of fresh flowers and gardens as they cover this beautiful quilt. This design will add artistry to everyday life.

You can bring the beauty of a colorful garden inside your home all year long with this eye-catching treasure.

instructions on pages 30 - 35

FABRIC USED: Sherbet
"Bali Pop" by *Hoffman*

Luscious orchid colors

Twist and turn

Turning another way

Twisting on a stone

Feeding the Koi fish

Offering flower petals

Royal water palace

FABRIC USED: Mulberry
"Bali Pop" by *Hoffman*

Twist and Turn

pieced by Donna Arrends Hansen
quilted by Julie Lawson

Bright colors, a bold pattern and memories of a fun-loving little girl dressed in a striped shirt inspired this attractive quilt. Her offering of food to the hungry fish brought her health and cheer.

Offerings play a significant role in Balinese life as they are believed to appease the spirits and thus bring prosperity and good health to the family. Bring warmth and cheer to your home.

instructions on pages 36 - 37

Praying at the temple

Bringing offerings

Respect to the spirits

High Priest ceremony

Offerings to the spirits

Traditional offering

Bringing offerings

Weaving leaves

Offerings of fruit

Parasols for deities

Ceremony for ancestors

Blessings and Offerings

pieced by Donna Arrends Hansen
quilted by Sue Needle

Colorful patterns and color in this quilt are in harmony. The Balinese way of life and religion are intertwined. Beliefs underscore four means of devotion – worshipping through prayer or holy recitations, good deeds without expecting profit or reward, learning and helping for social benefit, and a path of aesthetic life.

Remember to count your blessings every day.

instructions on pages 38 - 40

FABRIC USED: Kiwiberry
"Bali Pop" by *Hoffman*

Women weave on looms.

Men tie off threads for Ikat.

Girls weave Ikat on looms.

Experienced Songket weaver

Spinning and sewing outside

FABRIC USED: Butterscotch
"Bali Pop" by *Hoffman*

Leaves of Gold

pieced by Janice Irick
quilted by Sue Needle

The rich hues of textiles, textures and plants thread through this leaf quilt. Dark and Light leaves are creatively pieced from strips of Batik fabric to create "Rob Peter to Pay Paul" designs.

You'll love this earthy quilt... something purposeful yet beautiful.

instructions on pages 41 - 43

BATIK & Inspired

Bouncing colors

Fabulous woven textures

Holding a Weaving

Antique Ikat fabrics

Metallic highlights

Exciting textures

Color Wheel in Red

pieced by Rose Ann Pegram
quilted by Julie Lawson

Dancing colors circle this exciting design. Strip piecing and small divider strips make the quilt a fast piecing technique.

instructions on pages 19 - 21

Color Wheels
Basic Instructions for Both Wheels

photos on pages 18 and 67

YARDAGE:
We used Batik fabrics from *Hoffman*

Purchase the following Batik fabrics:
Fabrics Needed to Make Both Wheels

Orange	½ yard
Red	½ yard
Purple	½ yard
Royal Blue	½ yard
Medium Blue	½ yard
Turquoise	½ yard
Lime for Rays	¼ yard
Black solid for Background, Rays & Borders	2½ yards

Sewing machine, needle, thread
'Fat Cat' template from *Wm. Wright* - EZ quilting
   (or a 60° quilter's ruler)
   This template makes cutting Wedge sections easy.

TIP: The yardage will make 2 color wheel centers.
   You will need to add borders to each quilt (page 21).

CUTTING INSTRUCTIONS for the WHEELS:
   Cut strips 2½" x the width of fabric from each color:
      4 Red
      4 Purple
      4 Royal Blue
      4 Medium Blue
      4 Turquoise
   Cut strips 1½" x the width of fabric from color:
      4 Orange
   Cut strips 7" x the width of fabric from color:
      8 Black 7" strips
   'Rays' - **Cut strips 1"** x the width of fabric from colors:
      8 Black
         Subcut into 24 Black strips, each 1" x 8".
         Subcut into 24 Black strips, each 1" x 6".
      4 Lime
         Subcut into 24 Lime strips 1" x 6".
   Cut 2 Black 3½" circles for the center of the Wheels.

SPECIAL INSTRUCTIONS - Each section is cut on the bias.
Sew and handle them carefully so they won't stretch.
It helps to stay-stitch along sides and the small edge of
   the Wheel to keep from stretching out of shape.
Use spray sizing on Wheel sections to keep from stretching.

Black

Turquoise
Medium Blue
Royal Blue
Purple
Red
Orange

Black

SEWING INSTRUCTIONS
   Line up the following strips into 4 sets of:
Black-Turquoise-Med. Blue-Royal Blue-Purple-Red-Orange-Black
   Sew the sets together side by side.
   Press. Make 4 strip-sets.

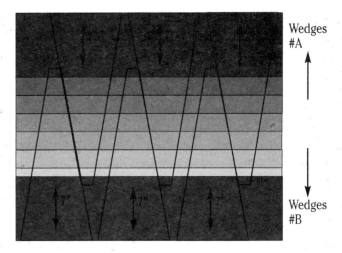

Wedges #A

Wedges #B

CUTTING the WEDGE SECTIONS:
   Lay out the strip-sets.
   With a 'Fat Cat' template (or 60° template quilt ruler),
      cut each strip-set into 6 Wedge sections (to make a
      total of 24 Wedge sections - 12 for each Wheel).
   Wedge Section #A - leave 7" of Black on the top (wide
      end), and 1" of Black on the bottom (narrow end).
   Wedge Section #B - leave 7" of Black on the bottom
      (wide end), and 1" of Black on the top (narrow end).

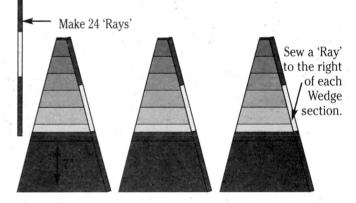

← Make 24 'Rays'

Sew a 'Ray' to the right of each Wedge section.

'RAYS' for the WEDGES:
   Sew the 1" strips of Black and Lime together end to
      end to complete 24 individual 'Rays':
      8" Black - 6" Lime - 6" Black. Press.
   Sew a 'Ray' to the right side of each Wedge section.
      (Be sure to be consistent on the side of the
      section that you sew the 'Ray' on.)

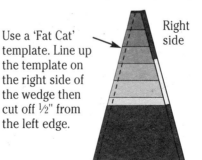

Use a 'Fat Cat' template. Line up the template on the right side of the wedge then cut off ½" from the left edge.

Right side

Before trimming   After trimming

TRIM the WEDGE SECTIONS:
   Trim each Wedge to fit the template.
   Use a 'Fat Cat' template (or 60° template quilt ruler).
   Line the template up along the Ray edge (on the right)
      and cut ½" off the opposite side (on the left).

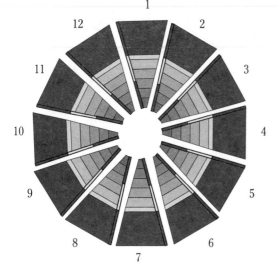

SEW the WEDGE SECTIONS TOGETHER:

Sew all 12 Wedge sections (either 12 "A" Wedges or 12 "B" Wedges) together to form one circle. Remember that you are sewing bias so handle the fabric pieces gently.

Applique a Black circle in the center.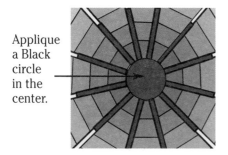

APPLIQUE the CENTER:

Applique a Black 3½" circle in the center of Wheel.

Color Wheel in Blue - Quilt Assembly Diagram

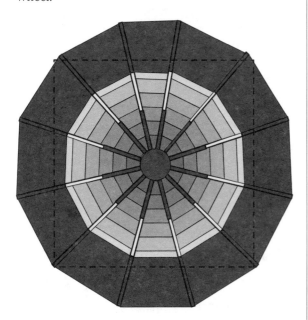

Color Wheel in Red - Quilt Assembly Diagram

SQUARE UP the WHEEL:

Square up the Color Wheel center to 27" x 27".

Refer to page 21 for finishing instructions.

Color Wheel in Blue
with Red-Orange Borders

photo on page 18

SIZE: 40" x 40"

To begin, refer to materials and instructions on page 19.

YARDAGE TO FINISH THE QUILT:

We used Batik fabrics from *Hoffman*

Purchase additional Batik fabrics for the border:

Border #2	Black is already purchased
Border #1, #3 & Binding	1⅙ yards Red-Orange mix
Backing	2 yards
Batting	48" x 48"
Sewing machine, needle, thread	

ADD THE BORDERS:
Border #1:
Cut Red-Orange strips 1¼" by the width of fabric.
    Cut 2 strips 1¼" x 27" for sides.
    Cut 2 strips 1¼" x 28½" for top and bottom.
    Sew side borders to the quilt. Press.
    Sew top and bottom borders to the quilt. Press.

Black Border #2:
Cut Black strips 2½" by the width of fabric.
    Cut 2 strips 2½" x 28½" for sides.
    Cut 2 strips 2½" x 32½" for top and bottom.
    Sew side borders to the quilt. Press.
    Sew top and bottom borders to the quilt. Press.

Border #3:
Cut Red-Orange strips 4½" wide parallel
    to the selvage to eliminate piecing.
    Cut 2 strips 4½" x 32½" for sides.
    Cut 2 strips 4½" x 40½" for top and bottom.
    Sew side borders to the quilt. Press.
    Sew top and bottom borders to the quilt. Press.

FINISHING:
Quilting: See Basic Instructions.
Binding: Cut strips 2½" wide.
    Sew together end to end to equal 170".
    See Binding Instructions.

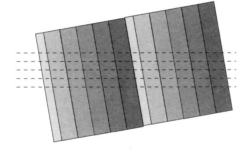

Color Wheel in Red
with Green-Lime Borders

photo on page 67

SIZE: 36½" x 36½"

To begin, refer to materials and instructions on page 19.

YARDAGE TO FINISH THE QUILT:

We used Batik fabrics from *Hoffman*

Purchase additional Batik fabrics for the border:

Border #1	Remnants from Color Wheel
Border #2 & Binding	Black is already purchased
Border #3	½ yard Green-Lime mix
Backing	1½ yards
Batting	45" x 45"
Sewing machine, needle, thread	

For Border #1 - Cut remnants diagonally 1½" wide from the leftover Wheel strip-sets.

ADD THE BORDERS:
Remnants Border #1:
Cut remnants diagonally from the leftover Wheel
    strip-sets to 1½" wide. Remove the Black ends
    then sew the color sections together end to end
    for the border strip.
    Cut 2 strips 1½" x 27" for sides.
    Cut 2 strips 1½" x 29" for top and bottom.
    Sew side borders to the quilt. Press.
    Sew top and bottom borders to the quilt. Press.

Black Border #2:
Cut Black strips 1" by the width of fabric.
    Cut 2 strips 1" x 29" for sides.
    Cut 2 strips 1" x 30" for top and bottom.
    Sew side borders to the quilt. Press.
    Sew top and bottom borders to the quilt. Press.

Border #3:
Cut Green-Lime mix strips 4" wide by the width of fabric.
    Cut 2 strips 4" x 30" for sides.
    Cut 2 strips 4" x 37" for top and bottom.
    Sew side borders to the quilt. Press.
    Sew top and bottom borders to the quilt. Press.

FINISHING:
Quilting: See Basic Instructions.
Binding: Cut strips 2½" wide.
    Sew together end to end to equal 156".
    See Binding Instructions.

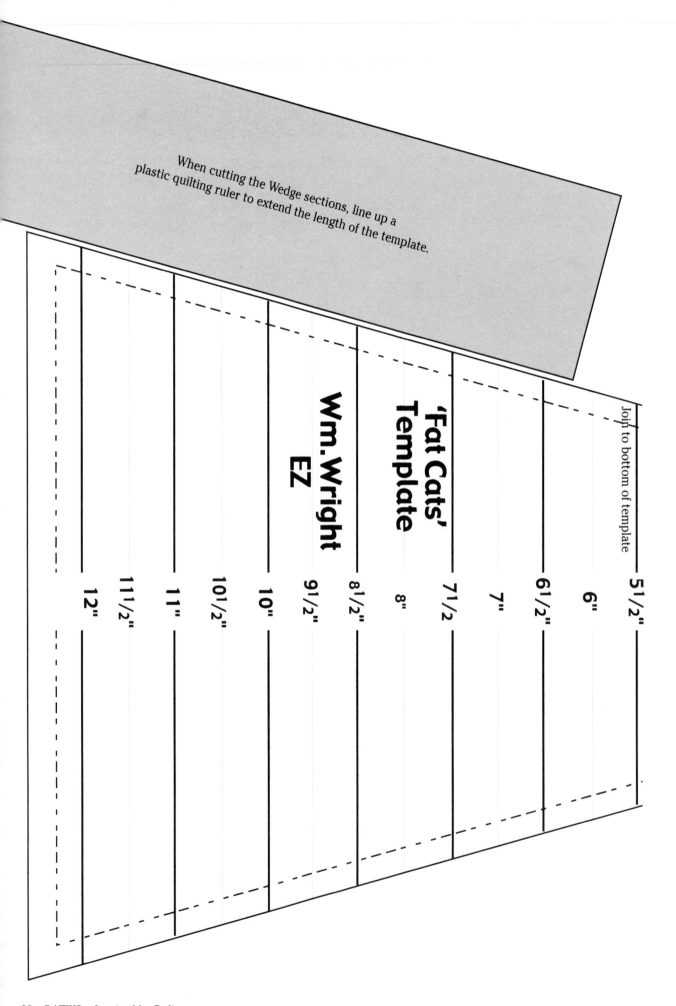

When cutting the Wedge sections, line up a
plastic quilting ruler to extend the length of the template.

Wm.Wright
EZ

'Fat Cats'
Template

Join to bottom of template

5¹/₂"

6"

6¹/₂"

7"

7¹/₂

8"

8¹/₂"

10"

9¹/₂"

10¹/₂"

11"

11¹/₂"

12"

Here is a drawing of the 'Fat Cat' template ruler by *Wm. Wright - EZ quilting.*
This plastic template makes cutting Wedge shapes easy.

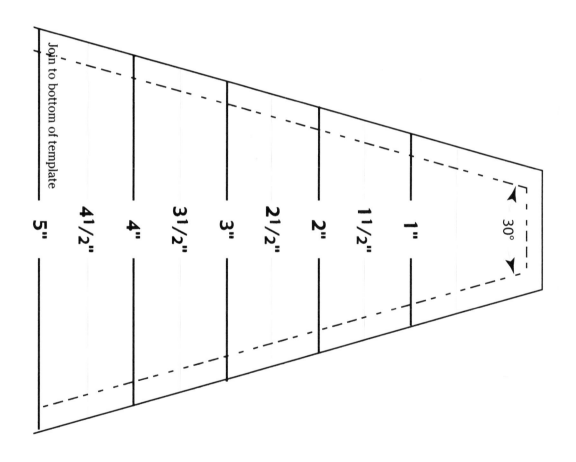

Sunrise

photo on pages 6 - 7

SIZE: 55" x 75"

YARDAGE:
We used a *Hoffman* Batik "Strawberry Fields - Bali Pop" collection of 2½" fabric strips
- we purchased 1 'Bali Pop'

10 assorted strips	OR	¾ yard Purple
8 assorted strips	OR	⅝ yard Tan/Gold/Cream
9 assorted strips	OR	⅝ yard Green/Turquoise/Teal
7 assorted strips	OR	½ yard Red/Rust/Purple/Brown
3 assorted strips	OR	¼ yard Brown/Green
2 assorted strips	OR	⅙ yard Black
1 strip	OR	⅛ yard Orange
Border #3		Purchase ⅜ yard Gold
Border #4 & Binding	Purchase 1⅞ yards Green/Rust	
Backing		Purchase 3½ yards
Batting		Purchase 63" x 83"

Sewing machine, needle, thread
Optional: "A Girl's Best Friend" Diamond Cut template ruler by *June Tailor*.
This plastic template makes cutting diamonds easy.

PREPARATION FOR STRIPS:
Cut all strips 2½" x 44".
Tip: Do not remove the selvage edge before cutting the diamonds. You need the entire 44" to make 8 diamonds. The selvage edge will be removed with the first and last cuts.
Label the stacks or pieces as you cut.

SORTING:
Refer to the sorting instructions on page 80.
Sort the 2½" strips into stacks by color.

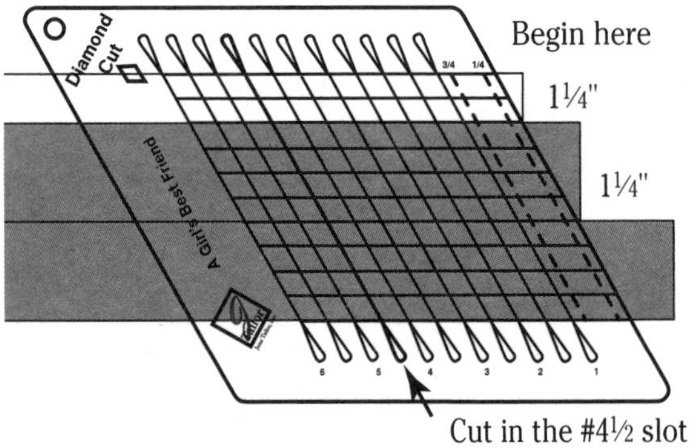

Begin here
1¼"
1¼"

Cut in the #4½ slot

Tips for Cutting with the Diamond Template -
You will use the same cut mark slot for both the Red and Orange diamonds.
Align the bottom line of the template with the edge of fabric strip-set bottom edge. Begin close to the right edge of strips. Make one diagonal cut on the right side to trim off the staggered ends.
Now place a rotary cutter in the #4½ slot and cut. You should have 1 diamond.
Move template to realign the right edge. Place rotary cutter in #4½ slot and cut again. You have 2 diamonds.
Repeat along the strip-set to make 8 diamonds.

POSITION	QUANTITY & COLOR
Red Diamonds	6⅓ Red/Rust/Purple/Brown
Gold Diamonds	8 Tan/Gold/Cream
Orange Corner Diamond	1 Orange
Sashing	10 Purple
Cornerstones	1 Black
Border #1	4 Brown/Green/Black
Piano Keys Border #2	A mix of the remaining strips

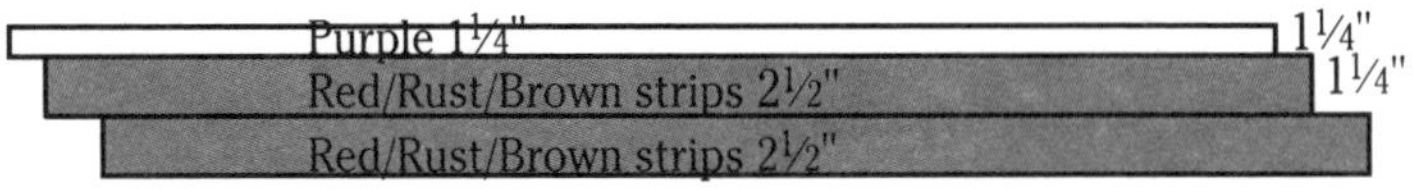

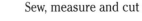

Purple 1¼"
1¼"
Red/Rust/Brown strips 2½"
1¼"
Red/Rust/Brown strips 2½"

Make 25 Red Diamonds with Purple Sashing:

Cut the Strips -
Cut 3 Purple Sashing strips 1¼" x 44".
Cut 6 Red/Rust/Purple/Brown strips 2½" x 44".

Cut one set of Short Strips -
Cut 1 Purple Sashing strip 1¼" x 7".
Cut 2 Red/Rust/Purple/Brown strips 2½" x 7".

Sew Strip-sets -
Sew the strips together side by side,
Purple - Red/Rust/Purple/Brown - Red/Rust/Purple/Brown
Be sure to stagger the strips from the **right side as shown**.
Press.
Make 3 long strip-sets plus 1 short strip-set.

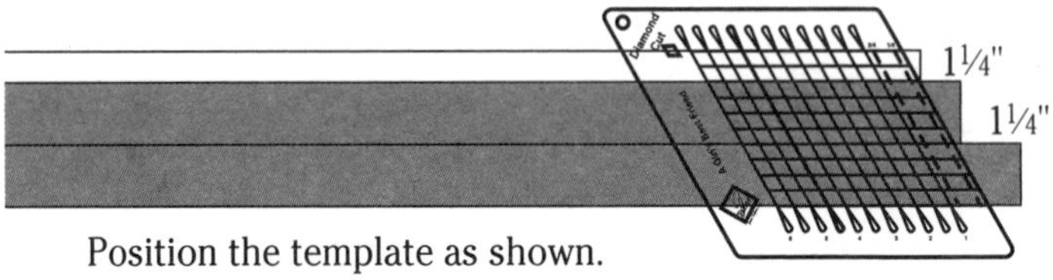

1¼"
1¼"

Position the template as shown.

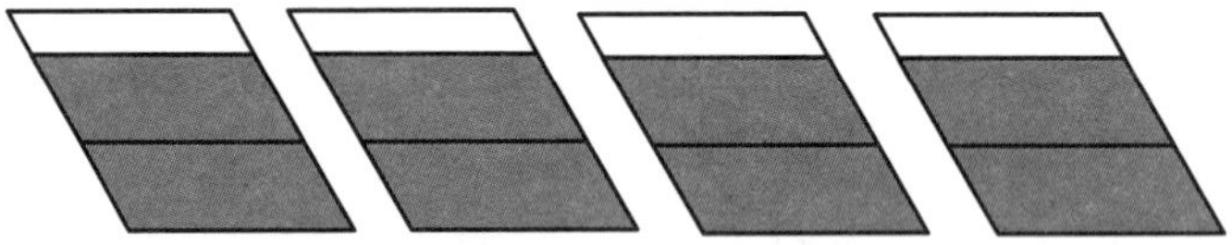
Cut a total of 25 Red diamonds.

Cut Diamond Shapes -
Cut each strip-set individually.
Position the ruler as shown.
Place the rotary cutter in the #4½ slot and cut.
Cut a total of 25 diamonds.
(Each 44" strip-set will yield 8 diamonds.)

Make 4 Orange Diamonds with Purple Sashing:

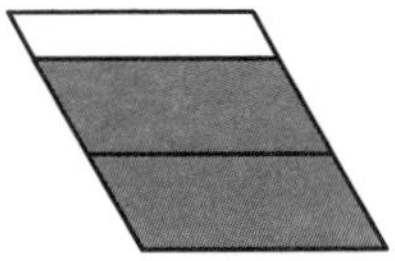

Cut one set of Strips -
Cut 1 Purple Sashing strip 1¼" x 22".
Cut 2 Orange strips 2½" x 22".

Sew Strip-sets and Cut Diamond Shapes –
Sew, measure and cut as above to make 4 diamonds. Press.

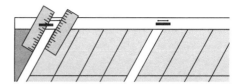

Make 32 Gold Diamonds
with Purple Sashing:

Cut the Strips -
Cut 4 Purple Sashing strips 1¼" x 44".
Cut 8 Tan/Gold/Cream strips 2½" x 44".

Sew Strip-sets -
Sew the strips together side by side,
Purple - Tan/Gold/Cream - Tan/Gold/Cream
Be sure to stagger the strips from the **right side as shown.**
Press. Make 4 strip-sets.

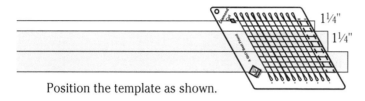

Position the template as shown.

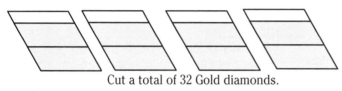

Cut a total of 32 Gold diamonds.

Cut Diamond Shapes -
Cut each strip-set individually.
Position the ruler as shown.
Place the rotary cutter in the #4½ slot and cut.
Cut a total of 32 diamonds.
(Each 44" strip-set will yield 8 diamonds.)

PREPARE SASHING STRIPS:
TIP: Because of the angles involved, the lengths given are longer than needed. The excess will be trimmed when the center is squared up.

Cut Sashing Strips -
Sashing A - Cut 4 strips 1¼" x 22".
Sashing B - Cut 4 strips 1¼" x 44".
Sashing C - Cut 2 strips 1¼" x 66".

Sewing Diamonds

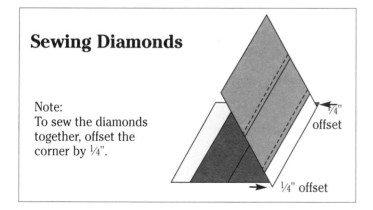

Note:
To sew the diamonds together, offset the corner by ¼".

¼" offset

¼" offset

ASSEMBLE THE ROWS:
Refer to diagram to the right for block placement.
Arrange all blocks in diagonal rows on a work surface.
Refer to the Sewing Diamonds diagram.
When sewing diamonds together, offset the edge by ¼".
Sew the diamonds for each row together.

Align Seams for Diamonds
Tips for Aligning Diamond Seams on Sashing:
If you have not sewn diamonds before, it can be a bit tricky to match the seams.
Refer to the diagrams.

Align Sashing Seams
Step 1:
On the right side of the sashing, draw lines with a chalk marker ¼" from the outer edge.
Align rulers or a straight edge with the sashing seams.
Make dots extending from the intersections, ¾" apart.
You will insert pins at these dots.

Step 2:
Position the pieced row on top of the sashing row, with right sides together.
Place pins ¼" from the outer fabric edge, aligning the marks with the short sashing seams.
Insert the pins through the dots you made in step 1.

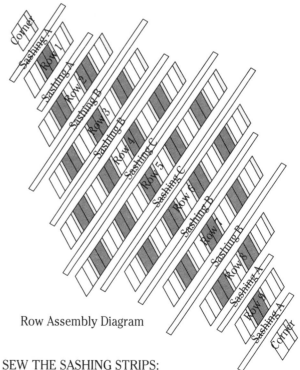

Row Assembly Diagram

SEW THE SASHING STRIPS:
Center and sew a 22" sashing to each side of row 1. Repeat for row 9. Press.
Center and sew 44" sashing to each side of row 3. Repeat for row 7. Press.
Center and sew 66" sashing to each side of row 5. Press.

QUILT ASSEMBLY:
Refer to the 'Align Seams for Diamonds' diagrams.
Pin and sew the rows together. Press.

Quilt Center

SQUARE UP THE QUILT CENTER:
Refer to the Quilt Center diagram.
Square up the quilt center to 27½" x 47½".

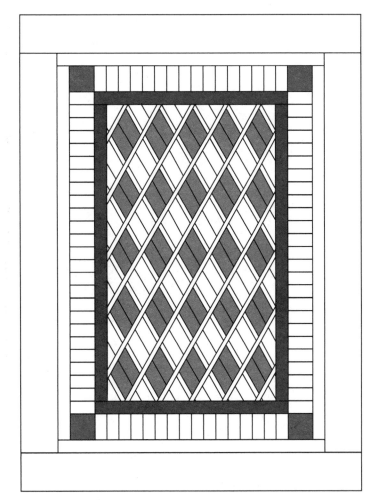

Sunrise - Quilt Assembly Diagram

BORDERS:
Border #1:
TIP: Cut 3 Brown/Green strips and 1 Black strip into 8" - 12" sections. Sew them back together end to end (this will create a scrappy look).
Cut 2 strips 2½" x 47½" for sides.
Cut 2 strips 2½" x 31½" for top and bottom.
Sew side borders to the quilt. Press.
Sew top and bottom borders to the quilt. Press.

Piano Keys Border #2:
Cut the remaining strips into 2½" x 9" lengths to make 42 pieces.
Sides:
Arrange 26 strips as desired.
Sew strips together side by side to make 9" x 52½":
Trim ½" off each end to make a piece 9" x 51½".
Cut the piece in half to make 2 pieces 4½" x 51½".
Top/Bottom:
Arrange 16 strips as desired.
Sew the strips together to make a piece 9" x 32½".
Trim ½" off each end to make a piece 9" x 31½".
Cut the piece in half to make 2 pieces 4½" x 31½".
Corners:
Cut 2 Black strips 2½" x 18".
Sew the strips together to make a piece 4½" x 18".
Cut the strip into 4 squares 4½" x 4½".
Sew a Corner square to each end of the
top and bottom borders. Press.
Assembly:
Sew side borders to the quilt. Press.
Sew top and bottom borders to the quilt. Press.

Border #3:
Cut 5 strips 2½" by the width of fabric.
Sew 3 strips together end to end.
Cut 2 strips 2½" x 59½" for sides.
Cut 2 strips 2½" x 43½" for top and bottom.
Sew side borders to the quilt. Press.
Sew top and bottom borders to the quilt. Press.

Border #4:
Cut strips 6½" wide parallel to the selvage to
eliminate piecing.
Cut 2 strips 6½" x 63½" for sides.
Cut 2 strips 6½" x 55½" for top and bottom.
Sew side borders to the quilt. Press.
Sew top and bottom borders to the quilt. Press.

FINISHING:
Quilting: See Basic Instructions.
Binding: Cut strips 2½" wide.
Sew together end to end to equal 270".
See Binding Instructions.

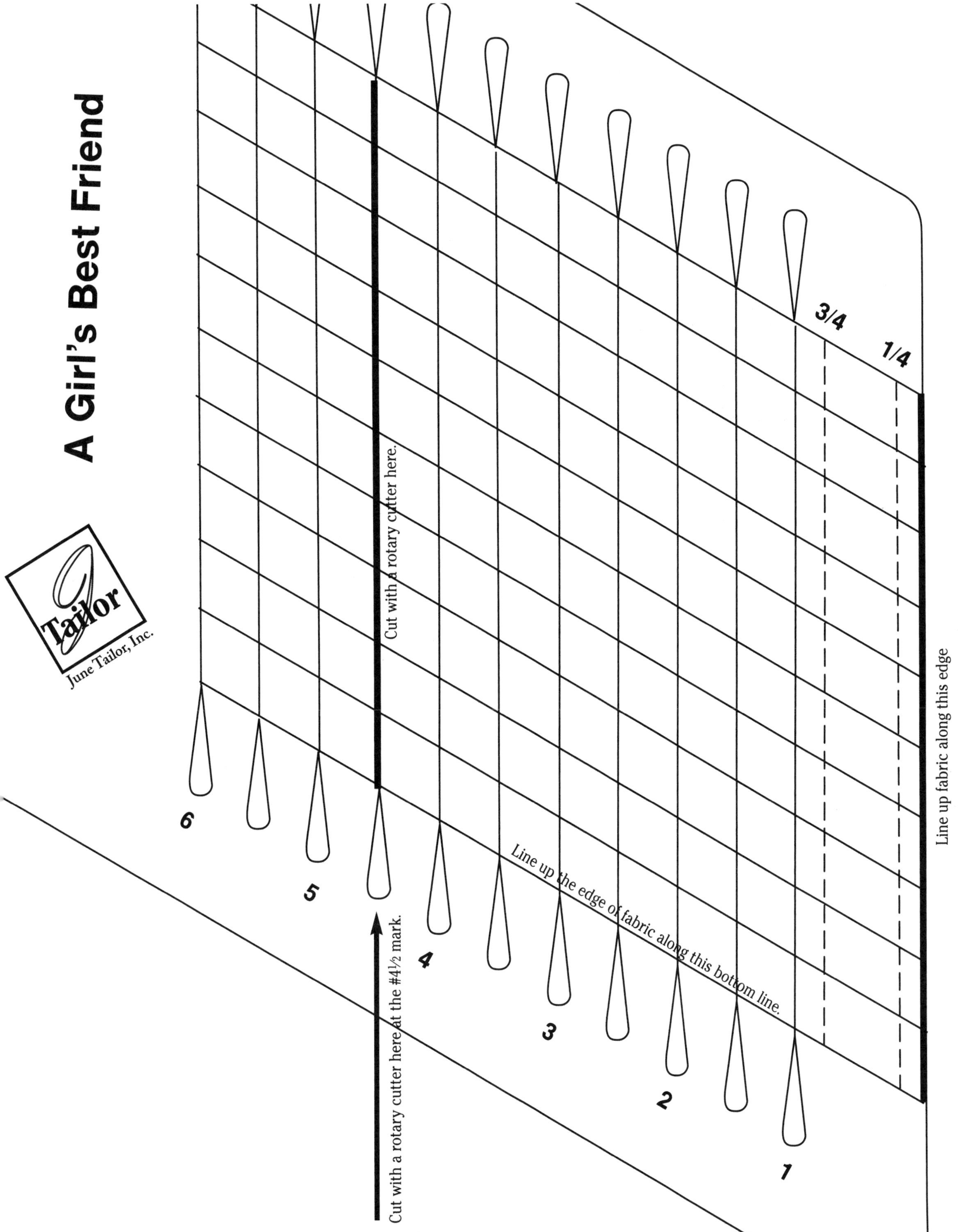

A Girl's Best Friend

June Tailor, Inc.

3/4

1/4

Cut with a rotary cutter here.

Line up fabric along this edge

Line up the edge of fabric along this bottom line.

Cut with a rotary cutter here at the #4½ mark.

6

5

4

3

2

1

Here is a drawing of 'A Girl's Best Friend' Diamond Cut template ruler by *June Tailor*.
This plastic template makes cutting accurate diamonds easy.

Emerald Forest

photo on pages 8 - 9

SIZE: 67" x 70"
TIP: Add more borders to make a larger quilt.

YARDAGE:
Yardage is given for using either fabric yardage
        or 'Bali Pop' 2½" strips.
We used a *Hoffman* Batik "Mint Chip - Bali Pop"
        collection of 2½" Batik fabric strips
        - we purchased 1 'Bali Pop'

10 assorted strips	OR	¾ yard Green
6 assorted strips	OR	½ yard Cream
5 assorted strips	OR	⅜ yard Light Blue
4 assorted strips	OR	⅓ yard Tan
5 assorted strips	OR	⅜ yard Dark Brown
6 assorted strips	OR	½ yard Purple
4 assorted strips	OR	⅓ yard Navy

Border #1	Purchase ¼ yard Dark Purple
Border #2	Purchase ½ yard Tan
Border #3 & Binding	Purchase 2 yards Green
Backing	Purchase 4⅛ yards
Batting	Purchase 75" x 78"

Sewing machine, needle, thread

PREPARATION FOR STRIPS:
        Cut all strips 2½" by the width of fabric
                (usually 42" - 44").
        Label the stacks or pieces by color as you cut.

SORTING:
        Refer to the sorting instructions on page 80.
        Sort the 2½" strips into stacks by color.

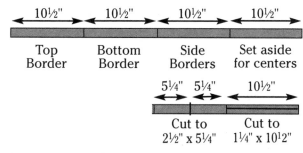

10½"	10½"	10½"	10½"
Top Border	Bottom Border	Side Borders	Set aside for centers

5¼"	5¼"	10½"
	Cut to 2½" x 5¼"	Cut to 1¼" x 10½"

CUT ALL STRIPS INTO THE FOLLOWING LENGTHS:
Cut every strip into 4 pieces 2½" x 10½".
Set one 2½" x 10½" piece aside for centers.

Border Strips -
Label one 2½" x 10½" piece 'top border'.
Label one 2½" x 10½" piece 'bottom border'.

side Borders -
Cut the last 2½" x 10½" piece into 2 pieces
        2½" x 5¼" and label them 'side strips'.

Center Strips -
        After all border strips are cut, refer to Cutting
chart to determine quantities and colors of center
strips. From strips labeled 'center', cut 39 center
strips, each 1¼" x 10½".

YOU WILL NEED THE FOLLOWING STRIPS:
Sort the cut strips into groups for each color of Block.

	Color	Quantity	Size		Center Strip	
A -	Green	16	2½" x 10½"	Tan	8	1¼" x 10½"
	Green	16	2½" x 5¼"			
B -	Light Blue	10	2½" x 10½"	Green	5	1¼" x 10½"
	Light Blue	10	2½" x 5¼"			
C -	Tan	10	2½" x 10½"	Green	5	1¼" x 10½"
	Tan	10	2½" x 5¼"			
D -	Green/Brown	4	2½" x 10½"	Green	2	1¼" x 10½"
	Green/Brown	4	2½" x 5¼"			
E -	Purple	12	2½" x 10½"	Cream	6	1¼" x 10½"
	Purple	12	2½" x 5¼"			
F -	Navy	6	2½" x 10½"	Brown	3	1¼" x 10½"
	Navy	6	2½" x 5¼"			
G -	Cream	10	2½" x 10½"	Navy	5	1¼" x 10½"
	Cream	10	2½" x 5¼"			
H -	Light Blue	2	2½" x 10½"	Navy	1	1¼" x 10½"
	Light Blue	2	2½" x 5¼"			
I -	Navy	2	2½" x 10½"	Green	1	1¼" x 10½"
	Navy	2	2½" x 5¼"			
J -	Dark Brown	6	2½" x 10½"	Green	3	1¼" x 10½"
	Dark Brown	6	2½" x 5¼"			

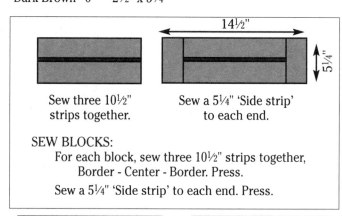

14½"   5¼"

Sew three 10½" strips together.

Sew a 5¼" 'Side strip' to each end.

SEW BLOCKS:
        For each block, sew three 10½" strips together,
                Border - Center - Border. Press.
        Sew a 5¼" 'Side strip' to each end. Press.

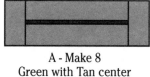

A - Make 8
Green with Tan center

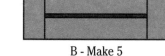

B - Make 5
Light Blue with Green center

C - Make 5
Tan with Green center

D - Make 2
Green/Brown with Green center

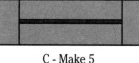

E - Make 6
Purple with Cream center

F - Make 3
Navy with Dark Brown center

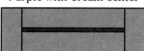

G - Make 5
Cream with Navy center

H - Make 1
Light Blue with Navy center

I - Make 1
Navy with Green center

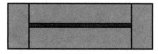

J - Make 3
Dark Brown with Green center

Cut the following blocks into 2 pieces 5¼" x 7¼" and label.

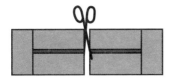

Cut 1 Block J - Dark Brown with Green

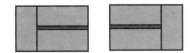

Cut 1 Block B - Light Blue with Green

Cut 1 Block F - Navy with Brown

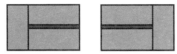

Cut 1 Block E - Purple with Cream

Cut 2 Block G - Cream with Navy
You will have one left over.

Emerald Forest - Quilt Assembly Diagram

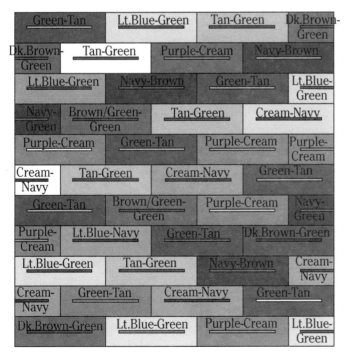

ASSEMBLY:
    Arrange all blocks on a work surface or table.
    Refer to diagram for block placement and direction.
    Sew blocks together in 11 rows,
        4 blocks per row. Press.
    Sew rows together. Press

BORDERS:
Border #1:
Cut 6 strips 1½" by the width of fabric.
Sew strips together end to end.
        Cut 2 strips 1½" x 52¾" for sides.
        Cut 2 strips 1½" x 51¼" for top and bottom.
        Sew side borders to the quilt. Press.
        Sew top and bottom borders to the quilt. Press.

Border #2:
Cut 6 strips 2½" by the width of fabric.
Sew strips together end to end.
        Cut 2 strips 2½" x 54¾" for sides.
        Cut 2 strips 2½" x 55¼" for top and bottom.
        Sew side borders to the quilt. Press.
        Sew top and bottom borders to the quilt. Press.

Border #3:
Cut strips 6½" wide parallel to the selvage to
        eliminate piecing.
        Cut 2 strips 6½" x 58¾" for sides.
        Cut 2 strips 6½" x 67¼" for top and bottom.
        Sew side borders to the quilt. Press.
        Sew top and bottom borders to the quilt. Press.

FINISHING:
Quilting: See Basic Instructions.
Binding: Cut strips 2½" wide.
            Sew together end to end to equal 288".
            See Binding Instructions.

Sunshine Garden

photo on pages 10 - 11

SIZE: 68" x 98"
TIP: Add more borders to make a larger quilt.

YARDAGE:
Yardage is given for using either Batik fabric
    yardage or 'Bali Pop' 2½" strips.
We used a *Hoffman* Batik "Sherbet - Bali Pop"
    collection of 2½" fabric strips
    - we purchased 1 'Bali Pop'

3 assorted strips	OR	¼ yard Medium Purple/Green
4 assorted strips	OR	⅓ yard Green
5 assorted strips	OR	⅜ yard Tan/Blue
6 assorted strips	OR	½ yard Pink/Green/Purple
5 assorted strips	OR	⅜ yard Light Blue/Aqua
3 assorted strips	OR	¼ yard Dark Purple/Blue
3 assorted strips	OR	¼ yard Light Pink/Light Green
6 assorted strips	OR	½ yard Coral/Purple
2 strips	OR	⅙ yard Lime
2 strips	OR	⅙ yard Turquoise

Quilt Center	Purchase 1⅛ yards Lime
Flower Appliques	Purchase ⅓ yard Dark Coral
Pitcher Applique & Stems	Purchase ⅓ yard Dark Blue mix
Borders #1, #4 & Applique	Purchase ¾ yard Light Blue
Border #3 & Applique	Purchase ⅞ yard Dark Blue
Border #5 & Binding	Purchase 2½ yards
Backing	Purchase 5⅞ yards
Batting	Purchase 76" x 106"

Sewing machine, needle, thread

PREPARATION FOR STRIPS:
    Cut all strips 2½" by the width of fabric
        (usually 42" - 44").
    Label the stacks or pieces as you cut.

SORTING:
    Refer to the sorting instructions on page 80.
    Sort the 2½" strips into stacks by color.

CUT THE CENTER:
Center Block of the Quilt:
    Cut a Lime rectangle 28½" x 38½".

CUTTING TIP:
Make 12 Block 1's first. This ensures that the longest
pieces are cut first.

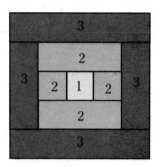

BLOCK #1 -
Make 12:
TIP:
    For each block, choose
2 pleasing strips.
    Cut strip and label them
#2 & #3. Assemble each
block as it is cut.
    Save leftovers for the
centers and assorted strips
on Block 2.

Blocks for the Quilt:
    Label the color stacks as you cut.
You will need 1 light color Pink strip for #1.
    (Use only 1 strip for all 12 center squares.)
    Cut 12 squares (total)   Center   (#1)   2½" x 2½"
You will need 6 medium color strips for #2.
    (Each block will use ½ strip.) For each block:
    Cut 2 squares   Position   (#2)   2½" x 2½"
    Cut 2 strips   Position   (#2)   2½" x 6½"
You will need 12 contrasting color strips for #3.
    (Each block will use 1 strip.) For each block:
    Cut 2 strips   Position   (#3)   2½" x 6½"
    Cut 2 strips   Position   (#3)   2½" x 10½"

Block #1 Assembly:
    Sew the center squares together: 2 - 1 - 2. Press.
    Sew Strip 2 (6½") to top and bottom of 2/1/2. Press.
    Sew Border 3 (6½") to each side of the piece. Press.
    Sew Border 3 (10½") to the top & bottom of piece. Press.

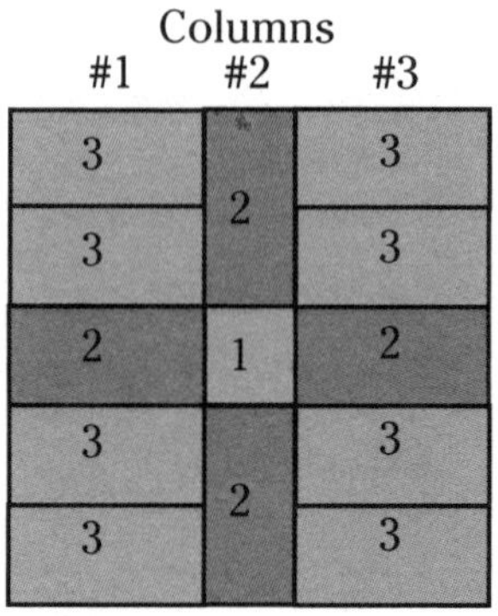

Columns
#1 #2 #3

BLOCK #2 -
Make 16:
TIP:
    For Block 2's you will
use all the remaining strips
and the leftover pieces
from Block 1.
    Choose 16 pleasing
color combinations before
cutting the strips or
sewing the blocks together.

Blocks for the Quilt:
    Label the color stacks as you cut.
You will need 7 strips for #2.
    (Each block will use ½ strip.) For each block:
    Cut 4 strips   Position   (#2)   2½" x 4½"
You will need 14 strips for #3.
    (Each block will use 1 strip.) For each block:
    Cut 8 strips   Position   (#3)   2½" x 4½"
Use assorted leftovers for the remaining 2 blocks. For each block:
    Cut 4 strips   Position   (#2)   2½" x 4½"
    Cut 8 strips   Position   (#3)   2½" x 4½"
Use leftovers from Block 1 to cut all 16 center squares #1.
    Cut 16 squares (total)   Center   (#1)   2½" x 2½"

Block #2 Assembly:
    Columns #1 & #3 - Sew strips together side by side:
        Sew 3 - 3 - 2 - 3 - 3. Press.
    Center Column #2 - Sew strips together end to end:
        Sew 2 - 1 - 2. Press.
    Sew the 3 columns together. Press.

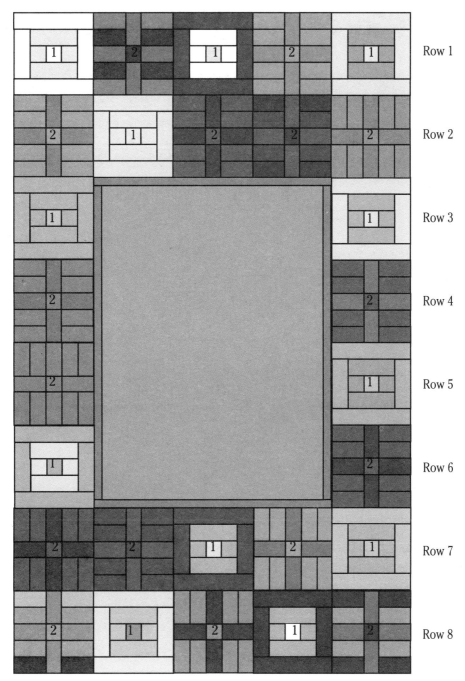

Row 1

Row 2

Row 3

Row 4

Row 5

Row 6

Row 7

Row 8

Blocks for Border #2

ASSEMBLY & BORDERS:

Border #1:
Cut strips 1½" by the width of fabric.
Sew strips together end to end.

 Cut 2 strips 1½" x 38½" for sides.
 Cut 2 strips 1½" x 30½" for top and bottom.
 Sew side borders to the quilt. Press.
 Sew top and bottom borders to the quilt. Press.

Blocks for Border #2:

Side Sections - Rows #3, #4, #5 & #6:
Sew Blocks 1-2-2-1 together to make a section 10½" x 40½".
 Press. Sew the section to the left of the Center. Press.
Sew Blocks 1-2-1-2 together to make a section 10½" x 40½".
 Press. Sew the section to the right of the Center. Press.

Top Section - Rows #1 & #2:
Sew Blocks 1-2-1-2-1 together to make a section 10½" x 50½".
 Press.
Sew Blocks 2-1-2-2-2 together to make a section 10½" x 50½".
 Press.
Sew the sections together. Press. Sew the section to the top
 of the quilt. Press.

Bottom Section - Rows #7 & #8:
Sew Blocks 2-2-1-2-1 together to make a section 10½" x 50½".
 Press.
Sew Blocks 2-1-2-1-2 together to make a section 10½" x 50½".
 Press.
Sew the sections together. Press.
Sew the section to the bottom of the quilt. Press.

OUTER BORDERS:

Border #3:

Cut 7 strips 1½" by the width of fabric.

Sew strips together end to end.

Cut 2 strips 1½" x 80½" for sides.

Cut 2 strips 1½" x 52½" for top and bottom.

Sew side borders to the quilt. Press.

Sew top and bottom borders to the quilt. Press.

Border #4:

Cut 7 strips 2½" by the width of fabric. Sew the strips together end to end.

Cut 2 strips 2½" x 82½" for sides.

Cut 2 strips 2½" x 56½" for top and bottom.

Sew side borders to the quilt. Press.

Sew top and bottom borders to the quilt. Press.

Border #5:

Cut strips 6½" wide parallel to the selvage to eliminate piecing.

Cut 2 strips 6½" x 86½" for sides.

Cut 2 strips 6½" x 68½" for top and bottom.

Sew side borders to the quilt. Press.

Sew top and bottom borders to the quilt. Press.

FINISHING:

Appliques: Refer to the Applique instructions.

Applique the pitcher, flowers, stems and birds in place as desired.

Beaks: Cut a 1½" square from a Tan strip for each beak.

Fold into a beak shape, place under the bird head and applique in place.

Quilting: See Basic Instructions.

Binding: Cut strips 2½" wide.

Sew together end to end to equal 342".

See Binding Instructions.

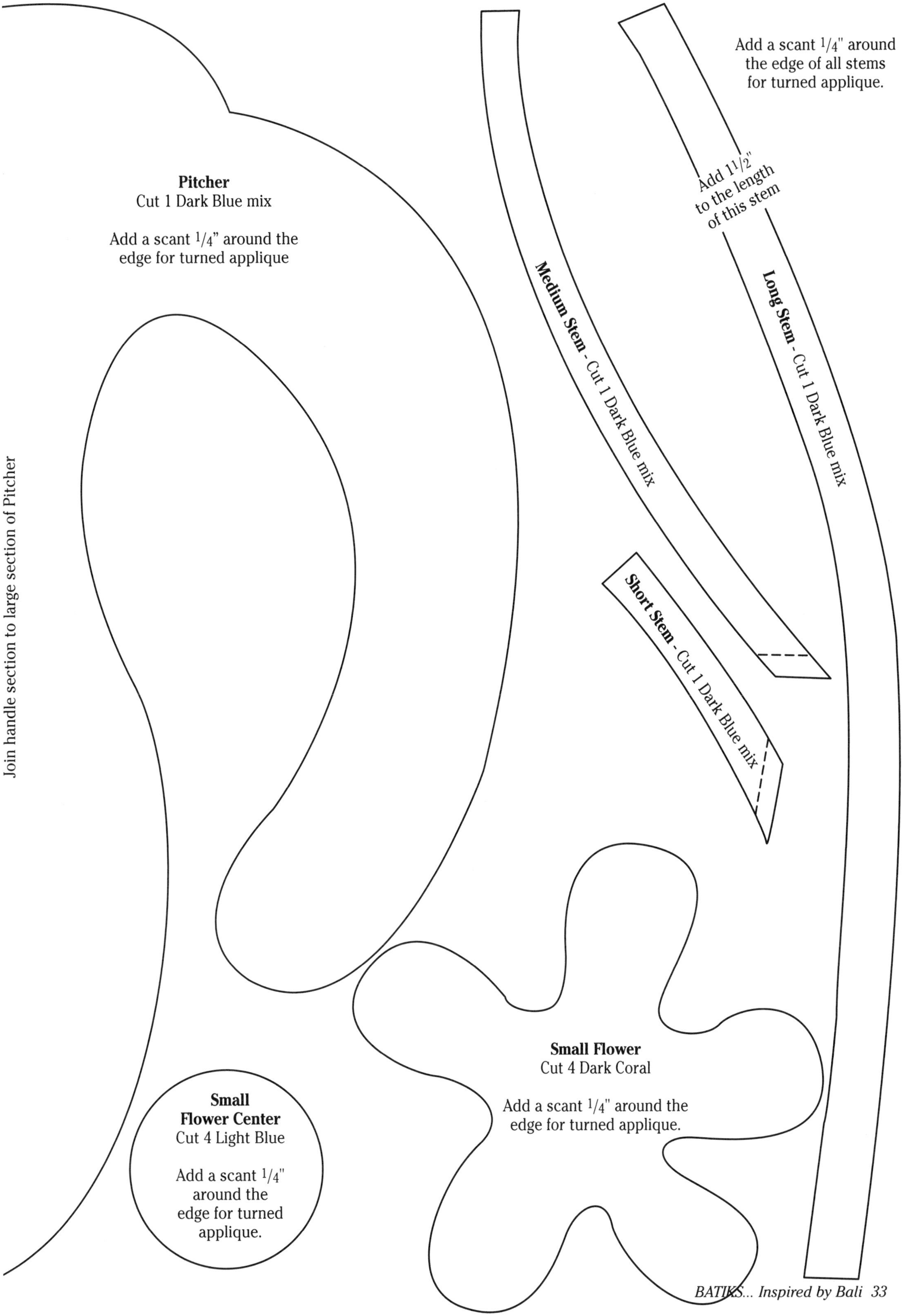

Pitcher
Cut 1 Dark Blue mix

Add a scant 1/4" around the
edge for turned applique

Join handle section to large section of Pitcher

Add a scant 1/4" around
the edge of all stems
for turned applique.

Add 1 1/2"
to the length
of this stem

Medium Stem - Cut 1 Dark Blue mix

Long Stem - Cut 1 Dark Blue mix

Short Stem - Cut 1 Dark Blue mix

Small Flower
Cut 4 Dark Coral

Add a scant 1/4" around the
edge for turned applique.

**Small
Flower Center**
Cut 4 Light Blue

Add a scant 1/4"
around the
edge for turned
applique.

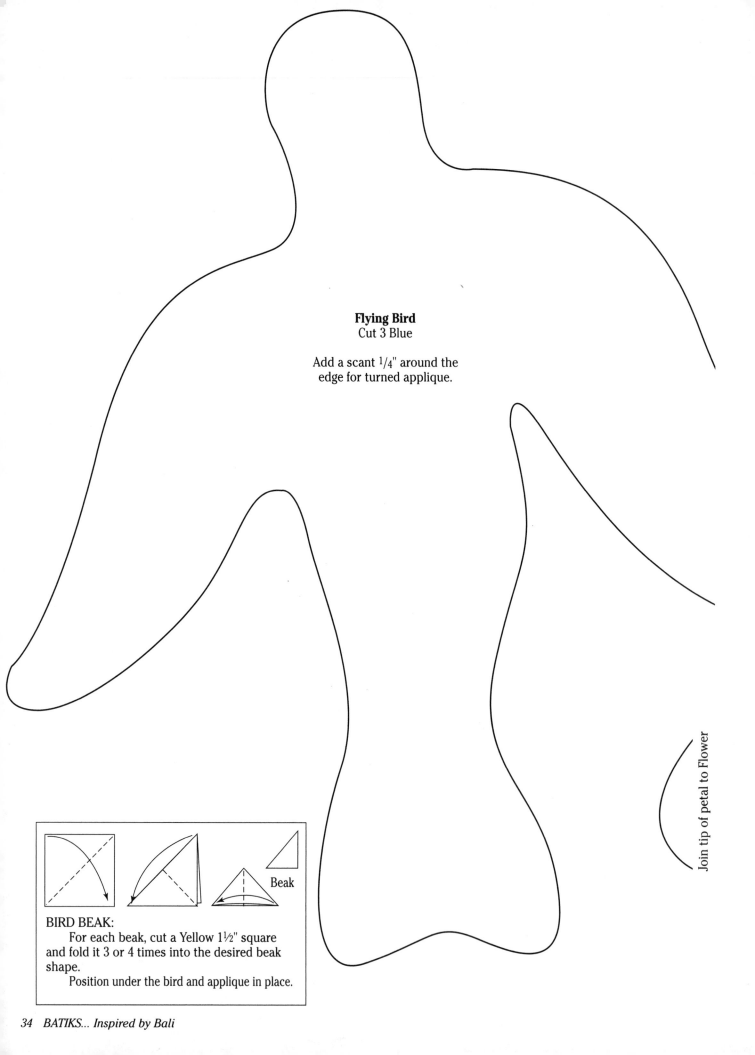

Flying Bird
Cut 3 Blue

Add a scant $1/4$" around the
edge for turned applique.

Join tip of petal to Flower

Beak

BIRD BEAK:
    For each beak, cut a Yellow $1\frac{1}{2}$" square
and fold it 3 or 4 times into the desired beak
shape.
    Position under the bird and applique in place.

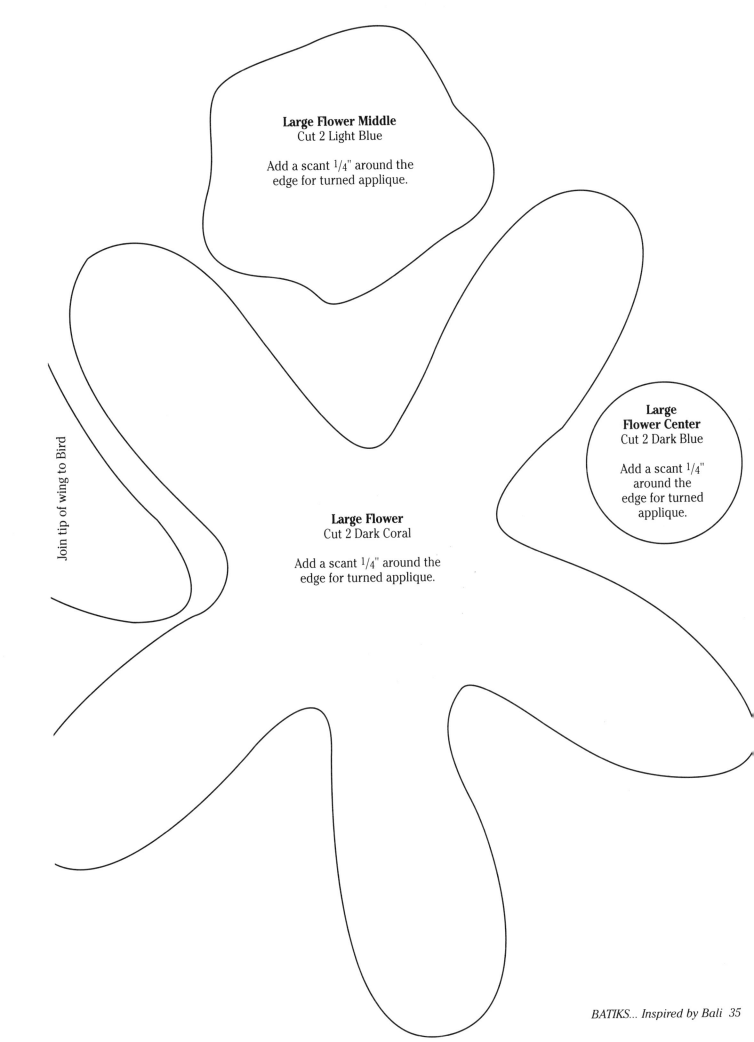

Large Flower Middle
Cut 2 Light Blue

Add a scant $1/4$" around the
edge for turned applique.

**Large
Flower Center**
Cut 2 Dark Blue

Add a scant $1/4$"
around the
edge for turned
applique.

Large Flower
Cut 2 Dark Coral

Add a scant $1/4$" around the
edge for turned applique.

Join tip of wing to Bird

Twist and Turn

photo on pages 12 - 13

SIZE: 72" x 84"
TIP: Add more borders to make a larger quilt.

YARDAGE:

Yardage is given for using either fabric yardage or
    'Bali Pop' 2½" strips.

We used a *Hoffman* Batik "Mulberry - Bali Pop" collection
of 2½" fabric strips - we purchased 1 'Bali Pop'

9 assorted strips	OR	⅔ yard Dark Purple-Green
9 assorted strips	OR	⅔ yard Dark Purple/Navy
7 assorted strips	OR	½ yard Medium Purple
5 assorted strips	OR	⅜ yard Tan
4 assorted strips	OR	⅓ yard Light Purple
4 assorted strips	OR	⅓ yard Cream
1 strip	OR	⅛ yard Lime Green
1 strip	OR	⅛ yard Bright Pink

Border #1 & Triangles	Purchase 1 yard Blue-Green
Border #2	Purchase ⅓ yard Lime
Border #3 & Binding	Purchase 2⅛ yards Purple
Backing	Purchase 5⅝ yards
Batting	Purchase 80" x 92"
Sewing machine, needle, thread	

PREPARATION FOR STRIPS:

Cut all strips 2½" by the width of fabric
    (usually 42" - 44").
Label the stacks or pieces as you cut.

SORTING:

Refer to the sorting instructions on page 80.
Sort the 2½" strips into stacks by color.

PREPARATION:

By taking the time to get organized now and
following a few simple steps, your quilt will be easy
to sew.

Separate your Strips by Color:

Place a sticky dot label or piece of masking tape
on the end of each strip, centering it between the
cut edges so that you can leave it in place until you
have finished sewing.

When working with Batiks, it can be difficult to
differentiate the colors. Mark the color of each strip
on the label, but write small because you will be
putting more information on each label.

Arrange Strips in Columns:

Arrange strips in two columns per the chart.
TIP: We made a few chevron rows 'match', but for
    most rows we chose a slightly darker color for
    the left side and a lighter color for the right side.

Left Side	Right Side
1. Dark Purple	1. Dark Purple
2. Tan	2. Dark Purple
3. Light Purple	3. Cream
4. Light Purple	4. Light Purple
5. Medium Purple	5. Light Purple
6. Dark Purple-Green	6. Dark Purple-Green
7. Dark Purple-Green	7. Dark Purple-Green
8. Tan	8. Cream
9. Dark Purple/Navy	9. Dark Purple
10. Dark Purple-Green	10. Tan
11. Bright Pink	11. Lime
12. Dark Purple	12. Dark Purple
13. Dark Purple	13. Medium Purple
14. Dark Purple	14. Medium Purple
15. Tan	15. Cream
16. Medium Purple	16. Medium purple
17. Medium Purple	17. Medium purple
18. Tan	18. Cream
19. Dark Purple-Green	19. Dark Purple-Green
20. Dark Purple-Green	20. Dark Purple-Green

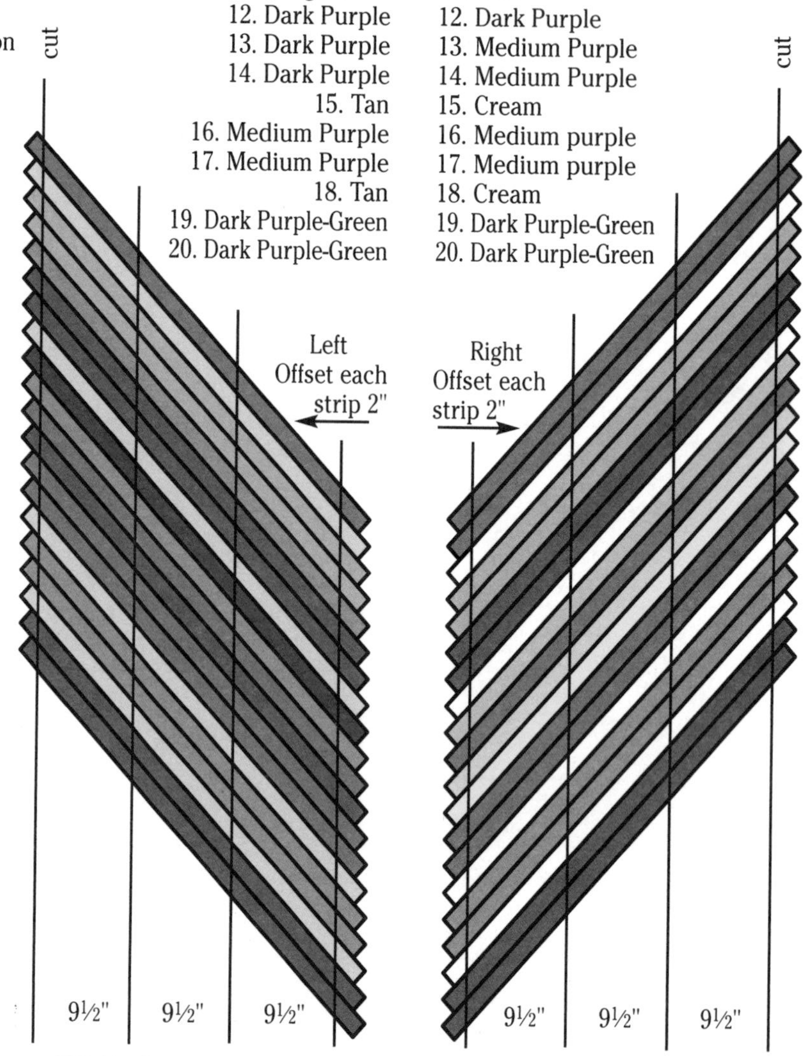

cut

Left
Offset each
strip 2" ←

Right
Offset each
strip 2" →

cut

9½"   9½"   9½"   9½"   9½"   9½"

TIP: On the sticky dot that you put on the strips, label each according
to its number in the sequence and placement (left or right).

TIPS FOR SEWING THE STRIP SETS:
Note: Strips are off-set row by row.
    Refer to the illustration above to **stagger the ends of the strips**.
    Sew one set of strips at a time.

Off-set (stagger) each strip by 2":
    Since the strips are not exactly the same length,
        always off-set the strips from the same end.

Sew strips together:
    Sew the strips together in pairs.
    Lay the strip pairs out in order on a work surface.
    Sew strip-sets together in pairs (this method will help the
        strip-sets lay flatter).
    Sew 10 pair.
    Repeat this process until the whole set is completely sewn together.
    Press the **right set** with all **seam allowances facing up**.
    Press the **left set** with all **seam allowances facing down**.

TIPS FOR CUTTING THE STRIP SETS:
Cut each strip set separately.
TIP: Once you cut the strip-sets you will be working with bias edges. Bias can stretch easily and needs to be handled gently.

CUTTING TIP:
Lay a strip-set flat on a cutting surface. Fold the bottom edge of strip-set up toward the top, matching the off-set points of the strips. Turn the strip-set so the folded edge is parallel to the edge of the cutting surface, closest to you. Carefully trim away the pointed ends on the strip-set to make a straight edge.

CUT 9½" SECTIONS:
Cut the strip-set into 3 sections
    9½" x the height of the strip-set.
Repeat with the second strip-set.

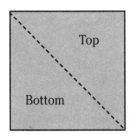 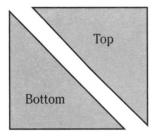

TOP AND BOTTOM TRIANGLES
Cut 6 Blue-Green squares 10" x 10".
Cut each square from corner to corner on the diagonal.
Sew the long side of the triangle (turn the triangle to fit)
    to the top and bottom edge of each strip-set.

Right side strips - Press the seam allowance
    toward the triangle.
Left side strips - Press the seam allowance
    toward the strip-set.

Section 1   Section 2   Section 3

ASSEMBLY:
Sew one left strip-set to one right strip-set.
Match the seams all the way down.
The seam allowances will fit snugly together. Press.

Repeat for the other two pairs of strip-sets. Press.
Sew two of the resulting sections together;
    then add the third section. Press.

Twist and Turn - Quilt Assembly Diagram

Note - Irrational Fractions:
Because the length of the diagonal on Border squares is an irrational number, the length of the quilt will have to be an unusual fraction. To avoid this problem, we have given you a little extra length on the borders and suggest trimming them to fit.

BORDERS:
Pieced Border #1:
Cut 7 strips 2½" by the width of fabric.
Sew strips together end to end.
    Cut 2 strips 2½" x 67½" for sides.
    Cut 2 strips 2½" x 58½" for top and bottom.
    Sew side borders to the quilt. Press.
    Sew top and bottom borders to the quilt. Press.

Border #2:
Cut 7 strips 1½" by the width of fabric.
Sew strips together end to end.
    Cut 2 strips 1½" x 71½" for sides.
    Cut 2 strips 1½" x 60½" for top and bottom.
    Sew side borders to the quilt. Press.
    Sew top and bottom borders to the quilt. Press.

Border #3:
Cut strips 6½" wide parallel to the selvage to eliminate piecing.
    Cut 2 strips 6½" x 73½" for sides.
    Cut 2 strips 6½" x 72½" for top and bottom.
    Sew side borders to the quilt. Press.
    Sew top and bottom borders to the quilt. Press.

FINISHING:
Quilting: See Basic Instructions.
Binding: Cut strips 2½" wide.
    Sew together end to end to equal 322".
    See Binding Instructions.

Blessings and Offerings

photo on pages 14 - 15

SIZE: 54" x 72"
TIP: Add more borders to make a larger quilt.

YARDAGE:
Yardage is given for using either fabric yardage or
    'Bali Pop' 2½" strips.
We used a *Hoffman* Batik "Bali Pop - Kiwiberry" collection
    of 2½" fabric strips - we purchased 1 'Bali Pop'

7 assorted strips	OR	½ yard Dark Purple
7 assorted strips	OR	½ yard Dark-Medium Blue
6 assorted strips	OR	½ yard Lime
5 assorted strips	OR	⅜ yard Dark Green
5 assorted strips	OR	⅜ yard Black-Teal
4 assorted strips	OR	⅓ yard Dark Blue-Lime
1 assorted strips	OR	⅛ yard Light Blue

Border #1	Purchase ⅜ yard Black
Mock Piping - Border #2	Purchase ¼ yard Lime
Border #3	Purchase ¼ yard Blue
Border #4 & Binding	Purchase 1¾ yards Black print
Backing	Purchase 4½ yards
Batting	Purchase 62" x 80"

Sewing machine, needle, thread

PREPARATION FOR STRIPS:
    Cut all strips 2½" by the width of fabric
        (usually 42" - 44").
    Label the stacks or pieces as you cut.

SORTING:
    Refer to the sorting instructions on page 80.
    Sort the 2½" strips into stacks by color.

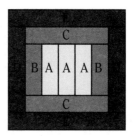

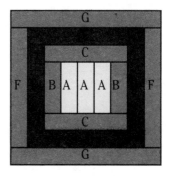

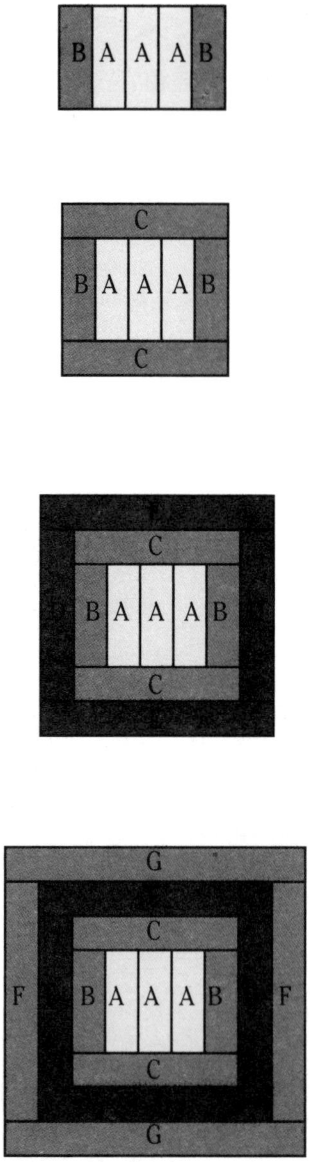

Courthouse Steps Block A -
Make 3.
For all 3 blocks you will need to cut:

Color	Quantity	Length	- Position
Lime	9	6½"	A
Dark Blue-Lime	6	6½"	B
	6	10½"	C
Black	6	10½"	D
	6	14½"	E
Dark Purple	6	14½"	F
	6	18½"	G

Assemble Block A:
    Sew 5 Center strips together: B - A - A - A - B.
Press.
    Sew strips C to top and bottom of block. Press.
    Sew strips D to the sides of the block. Press.
    Sew strips E to top and bottom of block. Press.
    Sew strips F to the sides of the block. Press.
    Sew strips G to top and bottom of block. Press.
Each block will measure 18½" by 18½" at this point.

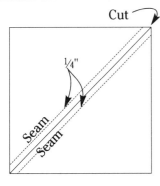

Half-Square Triangle Diagram

1. Place 2 squares right sides together.
2. Draw a diagonal line from corner to corner.
3. Stitch ¼" on each side of the line.
4. Cut squares apart on the diagonal line.
5. Open the 2 new squares with 2 colors.
6. Press. Trim off dog-ears.
7. Center and trim to size.

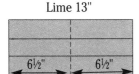
Lime 13"   6½"   6½"

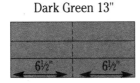
Dark Green 13"   6½"   6½"

Each pair of Dark Green-Lime squares makes 2 Half-Square Triangle blocks

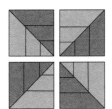

Pinwheel Block

Pinwheel Block B -

Make 3:

For these blocks, you will make the pinwheels first, add the purple border and then add the background triangles. For all 3 blocks you will need to cut:

Color	Quantity	Length
Dark Green	9	13"
Lime	9	13"

Assemble the Strip-sets:

Dark Green - Sew 3 strips together side by side. Press with all the seam allowances facing one direction. You will have a rectangle 13" by 6½". Cut this piece in half to create 2 squares 6½" by 6½".

Lime - Repeat this step with 3 Lime strips.

Assemble the Half square triangle blocks:

TIP: It is not necessary to match the interior seams.
Pair up the Dark Green and Lime squares.
Follow the instructions in the Half-Square Triangle diagram to make 12 half-square triangles.
Trim each block to 5¾" x 5¾".

Assemble the Pinwheel:

Arrange four half-square triangle blocks in a pinwheel.
Sew 2 rows of 2 blocks.
Press seam allowances in the opposite direction from each other.
Sew the two rows together. Press.
The assembled pinwheel will measure 11" x 11".

Sew the squares together then add the border

Add the Pinwheel Border:

Color	Quantity	Length
Dark Purple	3	11"
Dark Purple	3	13"

Cut both strips in half lengthwise to make
    6 strips 1¼" x 11" and 6 strips 1¼" x 12½".
Sew 11" strips to top and bottom of pinwheel. Press.
Sew 12½" strips to the sides of the pinwheel. Press.
The pinwheel will measure 13" x 13" at this point.

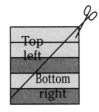 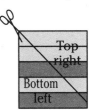

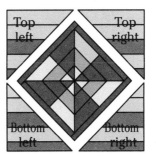 

Finished block

Add Background Triangles to Block B -

Make 3:

Color	Quantity	Length
Dark & Medium Blue	30	10½"

Assemble the Strip-sets:

Use 10 strips to make 2 units of 5 strips each.
Sew five strips together side by side. Press.
You will have two squares 10½" x 10½".

Cut both squares on the diagonal from corner to corner (note the direction of the diagonals). Press. Make a total of 4 triangles.

Sew a Triangle to each corner:

Sew the Top left and Bottom right triangles to opposite sides of the pinwheel. Press.

Sew the Top right and Bottom left triangles to remaining sides of the pinwheel. Press.

Trim and Make 2 more Blocks:

Once the background triangles are in place the block will need to be trimmed to size.
Trim the block to 18½" x 18½" at this point.
Repeat to make 2 more Pinwheel blocks.

Blessing and Offerings - Quilt Assembly Diagram

ASSEMBLY:
Arrange the 6 blocks on a work surface or table.
Refer to the diagram for block placement.
Sew the blocks together in 3 rows,
    with 2 blocks per row. Press
Sew the rows together. Press.

BORDERS:
Pieced Border #1:
Cut 5 strips 2½" by the width of fabric.
Sew 3 strips together end to end.
    Cut 2 strips 2½" x 54½" for sides.
    Cut 2 strips 2½" x 40½" for top and bottom.
    Sew side borders to the quilt. Press.
    Sew top and bottom borders to the quilt. Press.

Mock Piping (Narrow Lime Border #2):
Cut 5 strips 1" by the width of fabric.
Sew 3 strips together end to end.
Side Strips - Cut 2 strips 1" x 58½".
    Fold and press to ½" x 58½"
Top and Bottom - Cut 2 strips 1" x 40½".
    Fold and press to ½" x 40½"
TIP: Press mock piping strips in half lengthwise
    with wrong sides together. the right side of
    fabric will show on both sides.
Baste side strips to the quilt using a ⅛" seam
    allowance, placing raw edge to raw edge.
Baste top and bottom strips overlapping the
    corners of side strips.

Border #3:
Cut 5 strips 1½" by the width of fabric.
Sew 3 strips together end to end.
Cut 2 strips 1½" x 58½" for sides.
Cut 2 strips 1½" x 42½" for top and bottom.
Sew the side strips to the quilt.
Sew the top and bottom strips to the quilt.
TIP: The mock piping will be sandwiched between
    border #1 & border #3.
    Press the border away from the quilt but leave
    the mock piping flat against the first border.

Border #4:
Cut strips 6½" wide parallel to the selvage to
    eliminate piecing.
    Cut 2 strips 6½" x 60½" for sides.
    Cut 2 strips 6½" x 54½" for top and bottom.
    Sew side borders to the quilt. Press.
    Sew top and bottom borders to the quilt. Press.

FINISHING:
Quilting: See Basic Instructions.
Binding: Cut strips 2½" wide.
    Sew together end to end to equal 262".
    See Binding Instructions.

Leaves of Gold

photo on pages 16 - 17

SIZE: 56" x 72"
TIP: Add more borders to make a larger quilt.

YARDAGE:
Yardage is given for using either fabric yardage or
    'Bali Pop' 2½" strips.
We used a *Hoffman* Batik "Butterscotch - Bali Pop"
    collection of 2½" fabric strips
    - we purchased 1 'Bali Pop'

8 assorted strips	OR	⅝ yard Green-Blue-Brown mix
5 assorted strips	OR	⅜ yard Golden Brown
8 assorted strips	OR	⅝ yard Black/NAVY
4 assorted strips	OR	⅓ yard Medium Green
4 assorted strips	OR	⅓ yard Dark Green
3 assorted strips	OR	¼ yard Cream
3 assorted strips	OR	¼ yard Tan mix
2 assorted strips	OR	⅙ yard Medium Brown
2 assorted strips	OR	⅙ yard Light Green
1 strip	OR	⅛ yard Rust

Border #1	Purchase ⅜ yard Cream
Border #2 & Binding	Purchase 1¾ yards Brown
Backing	Purchase 4¼ yards
Batting	Purchase 64" x 80"

Sewing machine, needle, thread

PREPARATION FOR STRIPS:
    Cut all strips 2½" by the width of fabric
        (usually 42" - 44").
    Label the stacks or pieces as you cut.

SORTING:
    Refer to the sorting instructions on page 80.
    Sort the 2½" strips into stacks by color.

PREPARE THE APPLIQUE BLOCKS:
You will need the following strips
    3 Cream
    3 Tan mix
    1 Golden Brown
    1 Light Green
    2 Medium Green
Note: Each block is cut from 1 (same color) strip.
For each block, cut 4 strips 2½" x 8½" long.

Color	Quantity	Cut	Size
Cream	3	cut 12	2½" x 8½"
Tan	3	cut 12	2½" x 8½"
Golden Brown	1	cut 4	2½" x 8½"
Light Green	1	cut 4	2½" x 8½"
Medium Green	2	cut 8	2½" x 8½"

Note: The strips to these blocks must be appliqued
    before the strips are sewn together:

APPLIQUES:
    Refer to the Applique instructions.
    You will need 2 Black strips.
    Cut Black into 10 pieces, each 2½" x 8½" for applique pieces.
    Using the Leaves pattern (page 41), cut 20 applique pieces
        from the 10 Black pieces.

Note: Positive - Negative Design -
    Because this is a positive-negative design, you will cut
    each 2½" x 8½" Black strip into 2 curved sections
    and USE BOTH PARTS.

Applique - Position and applique the pair of 'leaves'
    to 2 strips of each background color.

Note: Turn Under the Curved Edge -
    On each applique, turn under the curved portion only
    and stitch it down on a background strip.

Note: Stitch Straight Edges into Seams -
    Align the straight raw edge of the applique with the
    edge of its background strip. Sandwich the raw edges
    of the applique in the seams as you sew. Press.

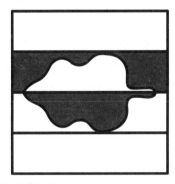

Complete Each Block -
    Sew 4 strips (2 with applique) together to complete
    each block. Press.
    Each block will measure 8½" x 8½" at this point.

PREPARE THE SOLID BLOCKS:
    You will need the remaining strips.
Note: Each block is cut from 1 (same color) 2½" wide strip.
For each block, cut 4 strips 2½" x 8½" long.

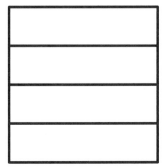

SEW BLOCKS:
    For each block, sew 4 strips together. Press.
    Each block will measure 8½" x 8½" at this point.

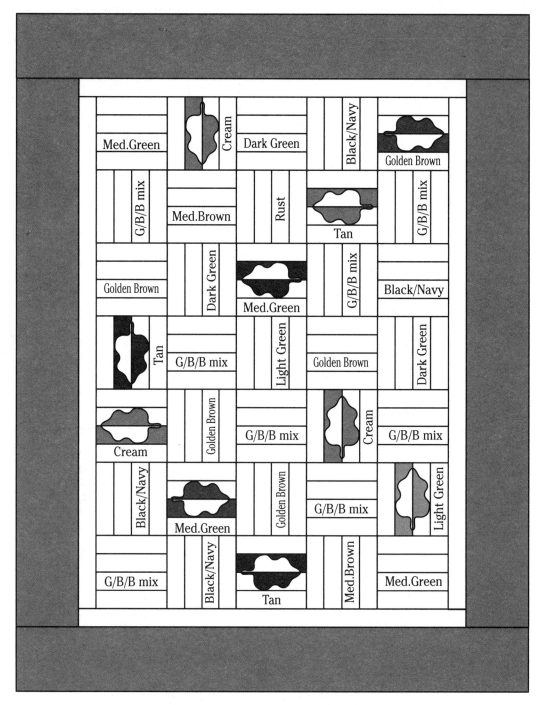

Leaves of Gold - Quilt Assembly Diagram

ASSEMBLY:
Arrange all blocks on a work surface or table.
Refer to diagram for block placement and direction.
Sew blocks together in 7 rows, 5 blocks per row. Press.
Sew rows together. Press.

BORDERS:
Border #1:
Cut 5 strips 2½" by the width of fabric.
Sew strips together end to end.
Cut 2 strips 2½" x 56½" for sides.
Cut 2 strips 2½" x 44½" for top and bottom.
Sew side borders to the quilt. Press.
Sew top and bottom borders to the quilt. Press.

Border #2:
Cut strips 6½" wide parallel to the selvage to
eliminate piecing.
Cut 2 strips 6½" x 60½" for sides.
Cut 2 strips 6½" x 56½" for top and bottom.
Sew side borders to the quilt. Press.
Sew top and bottom borders to the quilt. Press.

FINISHING:
Quilting: See Basic Instructions.
Binding: Cut strips 2½" wide.
Sew together end to end to equal 266".
See Binding Instructions.

Cut each 2½" x 8½" Black strip into 2 sections. Use both the left and the right parts.

On each applique, turn under the curved portion only.

Align the straight raw edges of the applique pieces with the edge of its background strip and stitch the applique right into the seam.

Applique the curved portion only.

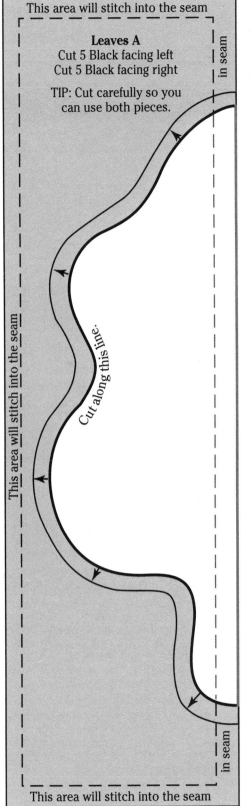

This area will stitch into the seam

Leaves A
Cut 5 Black facing left
Cut 5 Black facing right

TIP: Cut carefully so you can use both pieces.

in seam

This area will stitch into the seam

Cut along this line.

in seam

This area will stitch into the seam

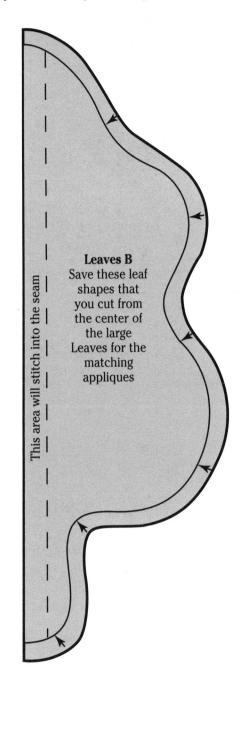

This area will stitch into the seam

Leaves B
Save these leaf shapes that you cut from the center of the large Leaves for the matching appliques

Leaves of Gold

Drenched in vibrant color, Leaves of Gold sizzles with the passion and movement of the tropics. Positive-negative appliqués create soft waves reminiscent of ocean breezes and the rustling of the leaves in the jungle canopy.

The Best Things About Batik 'Bali Pops'

I love to quilt, but it is often difficult to find time to cut and piece a quilt top. When I saw collections of Batik 2$\frac{1}{2}$" pre-cut fabric strips, I knew they were the answer.

No more spending hours choosing and cutting fabrics. Now I can begin sewing right away. Beautiful colors are available in every set. So whether I like jewel colors, heritage hues, soft pastels or earthy tones... there is an assortment for me.

Now my goals... a handmade cover for every bed, an heirloom quilt for each new baby and a pieced quilt for each of my children... are within reach. With 'Bali Pops' it is possible to complete a quilt top in a weekend.

After I piece all the blocks together, I use leftover strips for the borders and binding. Nothing really goes to waste and, if needed, I can purchase a bit of extra fabric for an extra punch of color or an additional yard for the border.

TIP: Quantities are given in strips and yardage so you know what you need and can start right away.

Tips for Working with Strips

Guide for Yardage:

2$\frac{1}{2}$" **Strips** - Each $\frac{1}{4}$ yard or a 'Fat Quarter' equals 3 strips

A strip cut from yardage or a pre-cut 'Bali Pop' strip is 2$\frac{1}{2}$" x 44"

Pre-cut strips are cut on the crosswise grain and are prone to stretching. These tips will help reduce stretching and make your quilt lay flat for quilting.

1. If you are cutting yardage, cut on the grain. Cut fat quarters on grain, parallel to the 18" side.

2. When sewing crosswise grain strips together, take care not to stretch the strips. If you detect any puckering as you go, rip out the seam and sew it again.

3. Press, Do Not Iron. Carefully open fabric, with the seam to one side, press without moving the iron. A back-and-forth ironing motion stretches the fabric.

4. Reduce the wiggle in your borders with this technique from garment making. First, accurately cut your borders to the exact measure of the quilt top. Then, before sewing the border to the quilt, run a double row of stay stitches along the outside edge to maintain the original shape and prevent stretching. Pin the border to the quilt, taking care not to stretch the quilt top to make it fit. Pinning reduces slipping and stretching.

Rotary Cutting

Rotary Cutter: Friend or Foe

A rotary cutter is wonderful and useful. When not used correctly, the sharp blade can be a dangerous tool. Follow these safety tips:

1. Never cut toward you.

2. Use a sharp blade. Pressing harder on a dull blade can cause the blade to jump the ruler and injure your fingers.

3. Always disengage the blade before the cutter leaves your hand, even if you intend to pick it up immediately.

Rotary cutters have been caught when lifting fabric, have fallen onto the floor and have cut fingers.

Basic Sewing

You now have precisely cut strips that are exactly the correct width. You are well on your way to blocks that fit together perfectly. Accurate sewing is the next important step.

Matching Edges:

1. Carefully line up the edges of your strips. Many times, if the underside is off a little, your seam will be off by ⅛". This does not sound like much until you have 8 seams in a block, each off by ⅛". Now your finished block is a whole inch wrong!

2. Pin the pieces together to prevent them shifting.

Seam Allowance:

I cannot stress enough the importance of accurate ¼" seams. All the quilts in this book are measured for ¼" seams unless otherwise indicated.

Most sewing machine manufacturers offer a Quarter-inch foot. A Quarter-inch foot is the most worthwhile investment you can make in your quilting.

Pressing:

I want to talk about pressing even before we get to sewing because proper pressing can make the difference between a quilt that wins a ribbon at the quilt show and one that does not.

Press, do NOT iron. What does that mean? Many of us want to move the iron back and forth along the seam. This "ironing" stretches the strip out of shape and creates errors that accumulate as the quilt is constructed. Believe it or not, there is a correct way to press your seams, and here it is:

1. Do NOT use steam with your iron. If you need a little water, spritz it on.

2. Place your fabric flat on the ironing board without opening the seam. Set a hot iron on the seam and count to 3. Lift the iron and move to the next position along the seam. Repeat until the entire seam is pressed. This sets and sinks the threads into the fabric.

3. Now, carefully lift the top strip and fold it away from you so the seam is on one side. Usually the seam is pressed toward the darker fabric, but often the direction of the seam is determined by the piecing requirements.

4. Press the seam open with your fingers. Add a little water or spray starch if it wants to close again. Lift the iron and place it on the seam. Count to 3. Lift the iron

again and continue until the seam is pressed. Do NOT use the tip of the iron to push the seam open. So many people do this and wonder later why their blocks are not fitting together.

5. Most critical of all: For accuracy every seam must be pressed before the next seam is sewn.

Working with 'Crosswise Grain' Strips:

Strips cut on the crosswise grain (from selvage to selvage) have problems similar to bias edges and are prone to stretching. To reduce stretching and make your quilt lay flat for quilting, keep these tips in mind.

1. Take care not to stretch the strips as you sew.

2. Adjust the sewing thread tension and the presser foot pressure if needed.

3. If you detect any puckering as you go, rip out the seam and sew it again. It is much easier to take out a seam now than to do it after the block is sewn.

Sewing Bias Edges:

Bias edges wiggle and stretch out of shape very easily. They are not recommended for beginners, but even a novice can accomplish bias edges if these techniques are employed.

1. Stabilize the bias edge with one of these methods:

a) Press with spray starch.

b) Press freezer paper or removable iron-on stabilizer to the back of the fabric.

c) Sew a double row of stay stitches along the bias edge and ⅛" from the bias edge. This is a favorite technique of garment makers.

2. Pin, pin, pin! I know many of us dislike pinning, but when working with bias edges, pinning makes the difference between intersections that match and those that do not.

Building Better Borders:

Wiggly borders make a quilt very difficult to finish. However, wiggly borders can be avoided with these techniques.

1. Cut the borders on grain. That means cutting your strips parallel to the selvage edge.

2. Accurately cut your borders to the exact measure of the quilt.

3. If your borders are piece stripped from crosswise grain fabrics, press well with spray starch and sew a double row of stay stitches along the outside edge to maintain the original shape and prevent stretching.

4. Pin the border to the quilt, taking care not to stretch the quilt top to make it fit. Pinning reduces slipping and stretching.

Embroidery Use 24" lengths of doubled pearl cotton or 6-ply floss and a #22 or #24 Chenille needle (this needle has a large eye). Outline large elements.

Running Stitch Come up at A. Weave the needle through the fabric, making LONG stitches on the top and SHORT stitches on the bottom. Keep stitches even.

Applique Instructions

Basic Turned Edge

1. Trace pattern onto no-melt template plastic (or onto Wash-Away Tear-Away Stabilizer).

2. Cut out the fabric shape leaving a scant $1/4$" fabric border all around and clip the curves.

3. **Plastic Template Method** - Place plastic shape on the wrong side of the fabric. Spray edges with starch. Press a $1/4$" border over the edge of the template plastic with the tip of a hot iron. Press firmly.

   Stabilizer Method - Place stabilizer shape on the wrong side of the fabric. Use a glue stick to press a $1/4$" border over the edge of the stabilizer securing it with the glue stick. Press firmly.

5. Remove the template, maintaining the folded edge on the back of the fabric.

6. Position the shape on the quilt and Blindstitch in place.

Basic Turned Edge by Hand

1. Cut out the shape leaving a $1/4$" fabric border all around.

2. Baste the shapes to the quilt, keeping the basting stitches away from the edge of the fabric.

3. Begin with all areas that are under other layers and work to the topmost layer.

4. For an area no more than 2" ahead of where you are working, trim to $1/8$" and clip the curves.

5. Using the needle, roll the edge under and sew tiny Blindstitches to secure.

Using Fusible Web for Iron-on Applique:

1. Trace pattern onto Steam a Seam 2 fusible web.

2. Press the patterns onto the wrong side of fabric.

3. Cut out patterns exactly on the drawn line.

4. Score web paper with a pin, then remove the paper.

5. Position the fabric, fusible side down, on the quilt. Press with a hot iron following the fusible web manufacturer's instructions.

6. Stitch around the edge by hand.

Optional: Stabilize the wrong side of the fabric with your favorite stabilizer.

Use a size 80 machine embroidery needle. Fill the bobbin with lightweight basting thread and thread machine with machine embroidery thread that complements the color being appliqued.

Set your machine for a Zigzag stitch and adjust the thread tension if needed. Use a scrap to experiment with different stitch widths and lengths until you find the one you like best.

Sew slowly.

Basic Layering Instructions

Marking Your Quilt:

If you choose to mark your quilt for hand or machine quilting, it is much easier to do so before layering. Press your quilt before you begin. Here are some handy tips regarding marking.

1. A disappearing pen may vanish before you finish.

2. Use a White pencil on dark fabrics.

3. If using a washable Blue pen, remember that pressing may make the pen permanent.

Pieced Backings:

1. Press the backing fabric before measuring.

2. If possible cut backing fabrics on grain, parallel to the selvage edges.

3. Piece 3 parts rather than 2 whenever possible, sewing 2 side borders to the center. This reduces stress on the pieced seam.

4. Backing and batting should extend at least 2" on each side of the quilt.

Creating a Quilt Sandwich:

1. Press the backing and top to remove all wrinkles.

2. Lay the backing wrong side up on the table.

3. Position the batting over the backing and smooth out all wrinkles.

4. Center the quilt top over the batting leaving a 2" border all around.

5. Pin the layers together with 2" safety pins positioned a handwidth apart. A grapefruit spoon makes inserting the pins easier. Leaving the pins open in the container speeds up the basting on the next quilt.

Basic Quilting Instructions

Hand Quilting:

Many quilters enjoy the serenity of hand quilting. Because the quilt is handled a great deal, it is important to securely baste the sandwich together. Place the quilt in a hoop and don't forget to hide your knots.

Machine Quilting:

All the quilts in this book were machine quilted. Some were quilted on a large, free-arm quilting machine and others were quilted on a sewing machine. If you have never machine quilted before, practice on some scraps first.

Straight Line Machine Quilting Tips:

1. Pin baste the layers securely.

2. Set up your sewing machine with a size 80 quilting needle and a walking foot.

3. Experimenting with the decorative stitches on your machine adds interest to your quilt. You do not have to quilt the entire piece with the same stitch. Variety is the spice of life, so have fun trying out stitches you have never used before as well as your favorite stand-bys.

Free Motion Machine Quilting Tips:

1. Pin baste the layers securely.

2. Set up your sewing machine with a spring needle, a quilting foot, and lower the feed dogs.

Basic Mitered Binding

A Perfect Finish:

The binding endures the most stress on a quilt and is usually the first thing to wear out. For this reason, we recommend using a double fold binding.

1. Trim the backing and batting even with the quilt edge.

2. If possible cut strips on the crosswise grain because a little bias in the binding is a Good thing. This is the only place in the quilt where bias is helpful, for it allows the binding to give as it is turned to the back and sewn in place.

3. Strips are usually cut 2½" wide, but check the instructions for your project before cutting.

4. Sew strips end to end to make a long strip sufficient to go all around the quilt plus 4"- 6".

5. With wrong sides together, fold the strip in half lengthwise. Press.

6. Stretch out your hand and place your little finger at the corner of the quilt top. Place the binding where your thumb touches the edge of the quilt. Aligning the edge of the quilt with the raw edges of the binding, pin the binding in place along the first side.

7. Leaving a 2" tail for later use, begin sewing the binding to the quilt with a ¼" seam.

For Mitered Corners:

1. Stop ¼" from the first corner. Leave the needle in the quilt and turn it 90°. Hit the reverse button on your machine and back off the quilt leaving the threads connected.

2. Fold the binding perpendicular to the side you sewed, making a 45° angle. Carefully maintaining the first fold, bring the binding back along the edge to be sewn.

3. Carefully align the edges of the binding with the quilt edge and sew as you did the first side. Repeat this process until you reach the tail left at the beginning. Fold the tail out of the way and sew until you are ¼" from the beginning stitches.

4. Remove the quilt from the machine. Fold the quilt out of the way and match the binding tails together. Carefully sew the binding tails with a ¼" seam. You can do this by hand if you prefer.

Finishing the Binding:

5. Trim the seam to reduce bulk.

6. Finish stitching the binding to the quilt across the join you just sewed.

7. Turn the binding to the back of the quilt. To reduce bulk at the corners, fold the miter in the opposite direction from which it was folded on the front.

8. Hand-sew a Blind stitch on the back of the quilt to secure the binding in place.

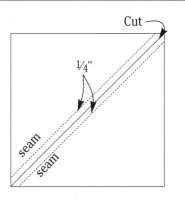

Half-Square Triangle

1. Place 2 squares right sides together.
2. Draw a diagonal line from corner to corner.
3. Stitch ¼" on each side of the line.
4. Cut squares apart on the diagonal line.
5. Open the 2 new squares with 2 colors.
6. Press. Trim off dog-ears.
7. Center and trim to size.

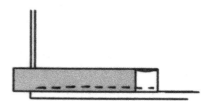

Align the raw edge of the binding with the raw edge of the quilt top. Start about 8" from the corner and go along the first side with a ¼" seam.

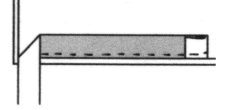

Stop ¼" from the edge. Then stitch a slant to the corner (through both layers of binding)... lift up, then down, as you line up the edge. Fold the binding back.

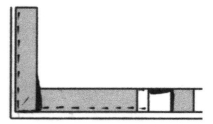

Align the raw edge again. Continue stitching the next side with a ¼" seam as you sew the binding in place.

Dancing Ladies

photo on pages 68 - 69

SIZE: 40½" x 46½"

YARDAGE:
We used Batik fabric by *Hoffman*

Purchase the following Batik fabrics:

Center Panel	1 panel 15" x 21"
Border #1 & 2	⅓ yard Lime
Triangles	⅛ yard Pink-Purple
Triangles & Corners	⅙ yard Violet
Border #3	¼ yard Green
Border #4	⅓ yard Purple
Border #5 & Binding	1⅓ yards Blue
Backing	2 yards
Batting	49" x 55"

Sewing machine, needle, thread

BATIK PANEL:
    We used a 15" x 21" Batik center panel.
    Suzanne made this one on her trip to Bali.
    Other prepared Batik panels are available from
        Bold Over Batiks
        St. Paul, MN
        boldoverbatiks.com

CUTTING FOR PANEL:
    Center panel: Cut 1 panel 15" x 21".

CUTTING FOR SNOWBALL CORNERS:

Color	Quantity	Size	Position
Lime	4	3½" x 3½"	Border
Violet	16	1¼" x 1¼"	Corners

CUTTING FOR BORDER:

Color	Quantity	Size	Position
Pink	10	4" x 4"	Border
Violet	10	4" x 4"	Border
Lime	4	3½" x 6½"	Border

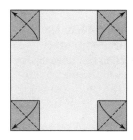 

MAKE 4 "SNOWBALL" SQUARES:
    Refer to the "Snowball" diagram.
    Align a Violet square with each corner.
    Draw a diagonal line from corner to corner.
    Sew on the line and fold back the triangle.
    Press.
    Repeat for all corners.
    Make 4.

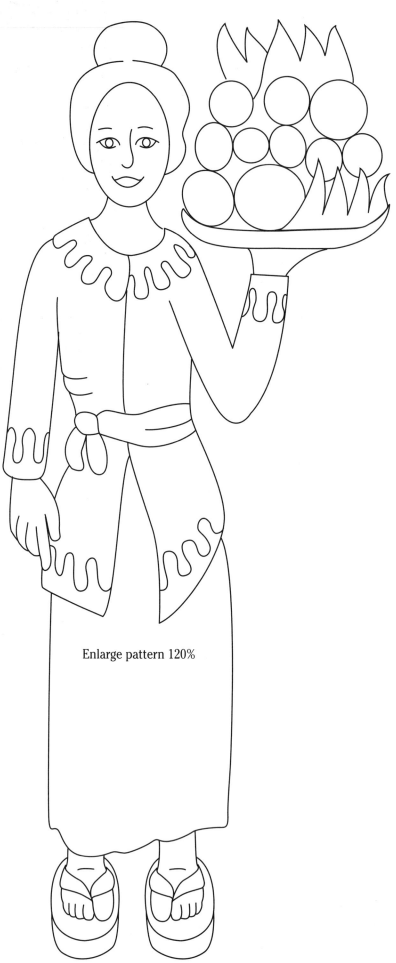

Enlarge pattern 120%

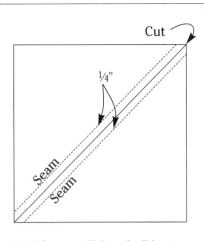

Half-Square Triangle Diagram
1. Place 2 squares right sides together.
2. Draw a diagonal line from corner to corner.
3. Stitch ¼" on each side of the line.
4. Cut squares apart on the diagonal line.
5. Open the 2 new squares with 2 colors.
6. Press. Trim off dog-ears.
7. Center and trim to size.

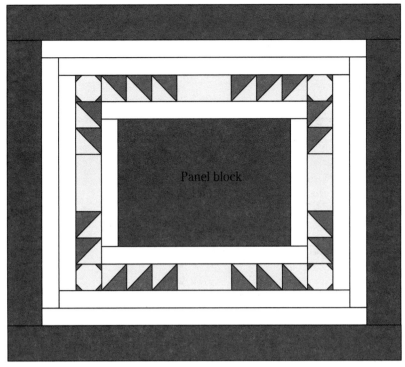

Dancing Ladies - Quilt Assembly Diagram

MAKE 20 HALF-SQUARE TRIANGLES:
   Pair up 10 Pink and Violet squares for the
      half-square triangles.
   Follow the instructions in the Half-Square Triangle
      Diagram to make 20 half-square triangles.
      Press.
   Trim each square to 3½" x 3½".

BORDERS:
Border #1:
   Cut 2 Lime strips 2½" x 15" for sides.
   Cut 2 strips 2½" x 25" for top and bottom.
   Sew side borders to the quilt. Press.
   Sew top and bottom borders to the quilt. Press.

Pieced Border #2:
   Side Borders:
   Refer to the Quilt diagram for placement.
   Sew the following together:
      2 half-square triangles -
      Lime rectangle -
      2 half-square triangles.
      Press. Make 2.
   Top & Bottom:
   Refer to the Quilt diagram for placement.
   Sew the following together:
      "Snowball"-
      3 half-square triangles -
      Lime rectangle -
      3 half-square triangles -
      "Snowball".
      Press. Make 2.
   Sew side borders to the quilt. Press.
   Sew top and bottom borders to the quilt. Press.

Border #3:
   Cut 2 strips 2½" x 25" for sides.
   Cut 2 strips 2½" x 35" for top and bottom.
   Sew side borders to the quilt. Press.
   Sew top and bottom borders to the quilt. Press.

Border #4:
   Cut 2 strips 2½" x 29" for sides.
   Cut 2 strips 2½" x 39" for top and bottom.
   Sew side borders to the quilt. Press.
   Sew top and bottom borders to the quilt. Press.

Border #5:
   Cut strips 4½" wide parallel to the selvage to
      eliminate piecing.
   Cut 2 strips 4½" x 33" for sides.
   Cut 2 strips 4½" x 47" for top and bottom.
   Sew side borders to the quilt. Press.
   Sew top and bottom borders to the quilt. Press.

FINISHING:
Quilting: See Basic Instructions.
Binding: Cut strips 2½" wide.
      Sew together end to end to equal 186".
      See Binding Instructions.

Elephant Walk

photo on pages 70 - 71

SIZE: 42" x 52"

YARDAGE:

We used Batik fabric from *Hoffman*

Purchase the following Batik fabrics:

3 Batik panels	3 panels 9" x 9"
Pinwheels & Border #1	⅜ yard Bright Blue
Pinwheels, Corners & Border #2	½ yard Coral
Block Borders & Corners	⅓ yard Red
Block Borders	⅙ yard Blue-Green
Border #1	⅛ yard Black
Border #3 & Binding	1¼ yards Blue leaf
Backing	2¼ yards
Batting	50" x 60"
Sewing machine, needle, thread	

BATIK PANEL:

    We used 3 Batik 9" x 9" panels.
    Suzanne made these on her trip to Bali.
    Other prepared Batik panels are available from
        Bold Over Batiks
        St. Paul, MN
        boldoverbatiks.com

CUTTING FOR PANEL:

    Cut 3 Batik panel squares 9" x 9".

MAKE BORDERS FOR PANELS:

    Cut 6 Red strips 1¼" x 9" for the sides.
    Cut 6 Red strips 1¼" x 10½" for the top & bottom.
    Sew side borders to each panel. Press.
    Sew top & bottom borders to each panel. Press.

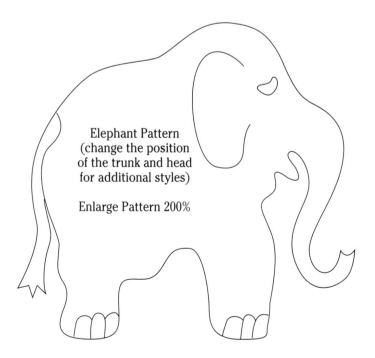

Elephant Pattern
(change the position
of the trunk and head
for additional styles)

Enlarge Pattern 200%

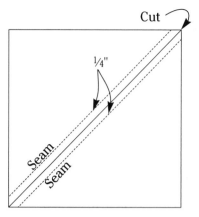

Cut

¼"

Seam

Seam

Half-Square Triangle Diagram
1. Place 2 squares right sides together.
2. Draw a diagonal line from corner to corner.
3. Stitch ¼" on each side of the line.
4. Cut squares apart on the diagonal line.
5. Open the 2 new squares with 2 colors.
6. Press. Trim off dog-ears.
7. Center and trim to size.

HALF-SQUARE TRIANGLES:

    Cut 6 Coral and 6 Bright Blue squares 6" x 6".
    Pair up 6 sets of Coral and Bright Blue squares.
    Follow the instructions in the Half-Square Triangle
        Diagram to make 12 half-square triangles.
    Trim each square to 4¾" x 4¾".

Row 1

Row 2

Make 3

PINWHEEL BLOCKS:

    Refer to the diagrams for placement.
    Sew the half-square triangles together with
        2 rows each, 2 blocks per row. Press.
    Sew the rows together. Press.

Add borders to 3

MAKE BORDERS FOR PINWHEELS:

    Cut 6 Green strips 1¼" x 9" for the sides.
    Cut 6 Green strips 1¼" x 10½" for the top & bottom.
    Sew side borders to each block. Press.
    Sew top & bottom borders to each block.
    Press.

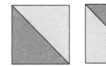

Make 2 Half-Square Triangles

Make 2 Squares aligning the seams

Draw a diagonal line   Hourglass Square

HOURGLASS BLOCKS FOR CORNERS:
Make Half-Square Triangle Squares:
Cut 2 Red squares 5½" x 5½".
Cut 2 Coral squares 5½" x 5½".
Pair up 2 sets of Red and Coral squares
Make 4 half-square triangles.

Make Hourglass Squares:
With right sides together and opposite fabrics facing one another, layer 2 half-square triangles together aligning the seam.

On the wrong side of the fabric, draw a diagonal line that crosses the seam.

Follow the procedure for making a half-square triangle.
Sew a ¼" seam on each side of the diagonal line.
Cut on the diagonal. Press.
Trim each block to 4½" x 4½".

MAKE PIANO KEYS FOR BORDER:
Sides:
Cut 8 Bright Blue strips 2½" x 9".
Cut 8 Black strips 2½" x 9".
Sew strips together side by side, alternating Blue and Black to make a piece 9" x 32½".
Trim 1" off each end to make a piece 9" x 30½".
Cut the strip into 2 pieces 4½" x 30½".

Top & Bottom:
Cut 5 Bright Blue strips 2½" x 9".
Cut 5 Black strips 2½" x 9".
Sew the strips together side by side, alternating Blue and Black to make a piece 9" x 20½".
Cut the strip into 2 pieces 4½" x 20½".

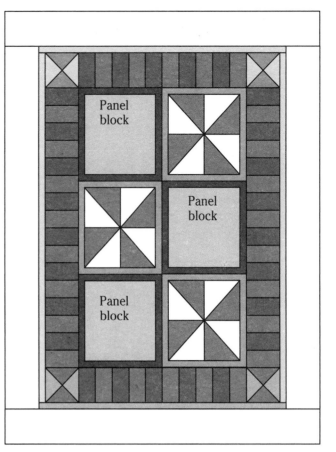

Elephant Walk - Quilt Assembly Diagram

ASSEMBLY:
Arrange all blocks on a work surface or table.
Refer to diagram for block placement.
Sew blocks together in 3 rows, 2 blocks per row. Press.
Sew rows together. Press.

Piano Keys - Border #1:
Sew side piano keys to the quilt. Press.
Sew an Hourglass Corner to each end of the top and bottom piano key strips.
Sew top and bottom piano keys to the quilt. Press.

Border #2:
Cut 2 strips 1½" x 38½" for sides.
Cut 2 strips 1½" x 30½" for top and bottom.
Sew side borders to the quilt. Press.
Sew top and bottom borders to the quilt. Press.

Border #3:
Cut strips 6½" wide by the width of fabric.
Cut 2 strips 6½" x 40½" for sides.
Cut 2 strips 6½" x 42½" for top and bottom.
Sew side borders to the quilt. Press.
Sew top and bottom borders to the quilt. Press.

FINISHING:
Quilting: See Basic Instructions.
Binding: Cut strips 2½" wide.
Sew together end to end to equal 198".
See Binding Instructions.

Village Square

photo on pages 72 - 73

SIZE: 64" x 74"

YARDAGE:

We used Batik fabrics from *Hoffman*

Purchase the following Batik fabrics:

Circle appliques & Border #4	¾ yard Red
Half-circle appliques	⅔ yard Blue-Green
Block A & Border #5	1⅙ yards Black
Borders #2 & #3	1 yard Bright Blue
Sashing & Border #1	½ yard Lime
Border #6 & Binding	1⅞ yards Black print
Backing	4 yards
Batting	72" x 82"
Sewing machine, needle, thread	
Circle templates (6" circle, 7" circle) from *June Tailor*	

CUTTING:

Block	Quantity	Color	Size
Block A	12	Black	8½" x 8½" squares
Circles	12	Red	6½" x 6½" squares
Vertical Sashes	8	Lime	2½" x 8½" strips
Horizontal Sashes	3	Lime	2½" x 28½" strips
Half-circles	11	Blue-Green	7½" x 7½" squares

APPLIQUE THE RED CIRCLES:
Refer to the Applique instructions.
Use the 6" circle template to cut
12 Red circles.
Applique 1 Red circle to each 8½" x 8½"
Black Block A. Press.

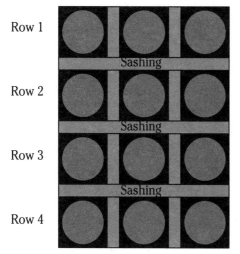

Row 1

Sashing

Row 2

Sashing

Row 3

Sashing

Row 4

ASSEMBLY:
Arrange all blocks and Sashing strips on a work surface or table.
Refer to diagram for block placement.
Sew the following for Row 1:
Block A - Vertical sashing - Block A - Vertical sashing - Block A.
Press.
Repeat for Row 2, Row 3 and Row 4.
Sew a Horizontal sashing to the bottom of Rows 1, 2, and 3.
Press.
Sew the rows together. Press.

BORDERS:

Border #1:
Cut Lime strips 2½" by the width of fabric.
Cut 2 strips 2½" x 38½" for sides.
Cut 2 strips 2½" x 32½" for top and bottom.
Sew side borders to the quilt. Press.
Sew top and bottom borders to the quilt. Press.

Border #2:
Cut Bright Blue strips 2½" by the width of fabric.
Cut 2 strips 2½" x 42½" for sides.
Cut 2 strips 2½" x 36½" for top and bottom.
Sew side borders to the quilt. Press.
Sew top and bottom borders to the quilt. Press.

Border #3:
Cut 3 Bright Blue strips 9" by the width of fabric.
Sew the strips together end to end. Press.
Cut 1 strip 9" x 46½" for sides.
Cut 1 strip 9" x 44½" for top and bottom.

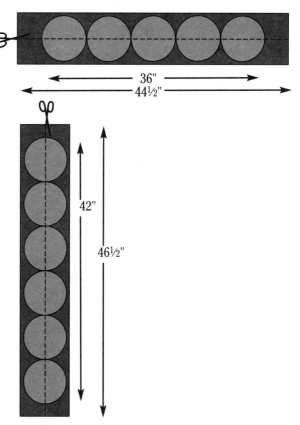

36"

44½"

42"

46½"

APPLIQUE THE BLUE-GREEN CIRCLES:
Refer to the Applique instructions.
Use a 7" circle template to cut 11 Blue-Green circles.
Applique 5 (evenly spaced) Blue-Green circles to
9" x 44½" strip for top and bottom borders.
Press.
Applique 6 (evenly spaced) Blue-Green circles to
9" x 46½" strip for side borders.
Press.

Cut Borders in Half:
Cut each Border strip in half lengthwise to make:
2 strips 4½" x 46½" for sides.
2 strips 4½" x 44½" for top and bottom.
Sew side borders to the quilt. Press.
Sew top and bottom borders to the quilt. Press.

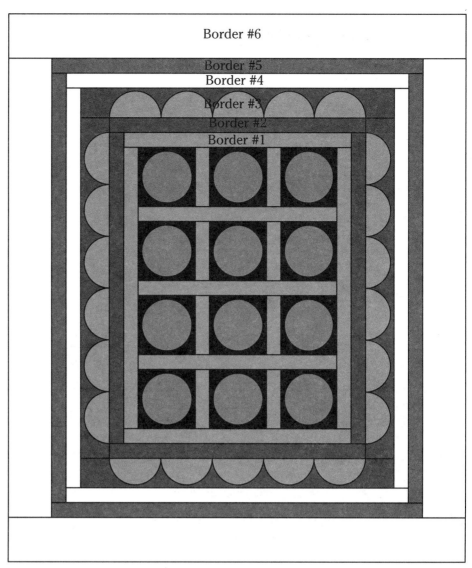

Village Square - Quilt Assembly Diagram

Border #4:
Cut 5 strips 2½" by the width of fabric.
Sew the strips together end to end. Press.
    Cut 2 strips 2½" x 54½" for sides.
    Cut 2 strips 2½" x 48½" for top and bottom.
    Sew side borders to the quilt. Press.
    Sew top and bottom borders to the quilt. Press.

Border #5:
Cut 6 strips 2½" by the width of fabric.
Sew the strips together end to end. Press.
    Cut 2 strips 2½" x 58½" for sides.
    Cut 2 strips 2½" x 52½" for top and bottom.
    Sew side borders to the quilt. Press.
    Sew top and bottom borders to the quilt. Press.

Border #6:
Cut strips 6½" wide parallel to the selvage to eliminate piecing.
    Cut 2 strips 6½" x 62½" for sides.
    Cut 2 strips 4½" x 64½" for top and bottom.
    Sew side borders to the quilt. Press.
    Sew top and bottom borders to the quilt. Press.

FINISHING:
Quilting: See Basic Instructions.
Binding: Cut strips 2½" wide.
    Sew together end to end to equal 286".
    See Binding Instructions.

Baskets & Sarongs

photo on pages 74 - 75

SIZE: 60" x 68"

YARDAGE:

We used Batik fabrics from *Hoffman*

Purchase the following Batik fabrics:

Center	⅞ yard Light Blue
Pinwheels	¾ yard Navy
Pinwheels & Sarongs	1 yard Pink
Baskets & Borders #1 & 3	⅝ yard Lime
Border #4	⅜ yards Dark Purple
Border #5 & Binding	1⅝ yards Light Purple-Green
Backing	3⅝ yards
Batting	68" x 76"

Sewing machine, needle, thread

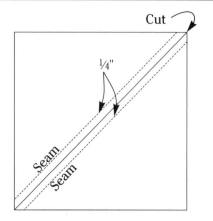

Half-Square Triangle Diagram
1. Place 2 squares right sides together.
2. Draw a diagonal line from corner to corner.
3. Stitch ¼" on each side of the line.
4. Cut squares apart on the diagonal line.
5. Open the 2 new squares with 2 colors.
6. Press. Trim off dog-ears.
7. Center and trim to size.

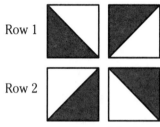

Row 1

Row 2

Assemble 4
Half Square Triangles

CENTER:
Cut 1 Light Blue rectangle 20½" x 28½".

APPLIQUE:
Refer to the Applique Instructions.
Use the patterns to cut out:
3 Baskets from Lime
3 Ladies in Sarongs from Pink
Applique as desired.

BORDERS:
Lime Border #1:
Cut 2 strips 2½" x 28½" for sides.
Cut 2 strips 2½" x 24½" for top and bottom.
Sew side borders to the Center. Press.
Sew top and bottom borders to the Center. Press.

PINWHEEL BORDER #2:
Half-Square Triangles:
Cut the following 5" x 5" squares:
36 Pink
36 Navy
Pair up 36 pairs of Pink - Navy squares for
half-square triangles.
Follow the instructions in the Half-Square Triangle
Diagram to make 72 half-square triangles.
Trim to 4½" x 4½".

Pinwheel Block

Assemble Pinwheels:
Refer to the Pinwheel diagram.
Arrange 4 half-square triangles in 2 rows of 2 squares each.
Sew the squares together. Press.
Sew the rows together. Press.
Each block will measure 8½" x 8½".
Make 18 blocks.

Baskets & Sarongs - Quilt Assembly Diagram

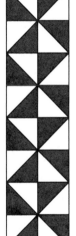

ADD PINWHEEL BORDER #2:
Refer to the Quilt Assembly diagram for block placement.
Side Borders:
> Sew 4 blocks together to make a strip 8½" x 32½".
> > Press. Make 2.
> Sew a strip to each side of the quilt. Press.

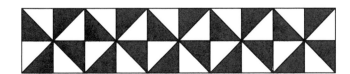

Top and Bottom Borders:
> Sew 5 blocks together to make a strip 8½" x 40½".
> > Press. Make 2.
> Sew a strip to the top and bottom of the quilt. Press.

SIDE BORDERS:
Lime Border #3:
Cut 5 strips 2½" by the width of fabric.
Sew strips together end to end.
> Cut 2 strips 2½" x 48½" for sides.
> Cut 2 strips 2½" x 44½" for top and bottom.
> Sew side borders to the quilt. Press.
> Sew top and bottom borders to the quilt. Press.

Dark Purple Border #4:
Cut 5 strips 2½" by the width of fabric.
Sew strips together end to end.
> Cut 2 strips 2½" x 52½" for sides.
> Cut 2 strips 2½" x 48½" for top and bottom.
> Sew side borders to the quilt. Press.
> Sew top and bottom borders to the quilt. Press.

Purple-Green Border #5:
Cut strips 6½" wide parallel to the selvage to
> eliminate piecing.
> Cut 2 strips 6½" x 56½" for sides.
> Cut 2 strips 6½" x 60½" for top and bottom.
> Sew side borders to the quilt. Press.
> Sew top and bottom borders to the quilt. Press.

FINISHING:
Quilting: See Basic Instructions.
Binding: Cut strips 2½" wide.
> Sew together end to end to equal 266".
> See Binding Instructions.

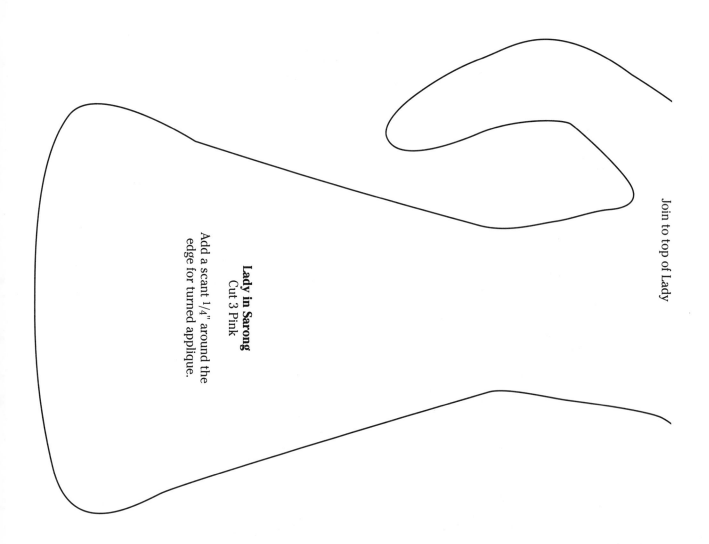

Lady in Sarong
Cut 3 Pink

Add a scant 1/4" around the
edge for turned applique.

Join to top of Lady

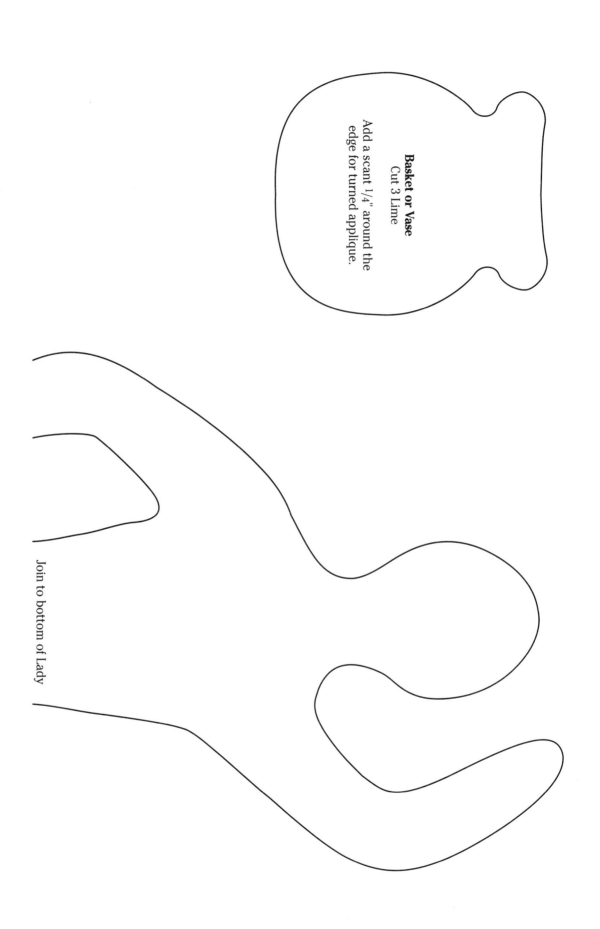

Basket or Vase
Cut 3 Lime

Add a scant 1/4" around the edge for turned applique.

Join to bottom of Lady

Keyhole

photo on pages 76 - 77

SIZE: 84" x 104"

YARDAGE:

We used Batik fabrics from *Hoffman*

Purchase the following Batik fabrics:

Center	½ yard	Lime
Round #1	1⅜ yards	Light Blue-Green
Round #2	3⅝ yards	Dark Blue-Green
Round #3 & Border	4¼ yards	Dark Blue
Backing	7½ yards	
Batting	92" x 112"	

Sewing machine, needle, thread

CUTTING:

Label the stacks or pieces by color as you cut.

Cut the following 3" strips for Checkerboards.

TIP: For longer strips, cut them parallel to the selvage to eliminate piecing and so they will be long enough.

CUT FOR A:

Light Blue-Green	2	3" x 48"	A
Lime	1	3" x 48"	A
Lime	2	3" x 24"	A
Light Blue-Green	1	3" x 24"	A

CUT FOR B:

Dark Blue	5	3" x 48"	B
Light Blue-Green	4	3" x 48	B

CUT FOR C:

Dark Blue-Green	5	3" x 72"	C
Dark Blue	4	3" x 72"	C

Cut the following 8" x 8" squares for Blocks:

Lime	3	8" x 8"	D
Light Blue-Green	12	8" x 8"	E
Dark Blue-Green	60	8" x 8"	F
Dark Blue	52	8" x 8"	G

Cut the following 6" x 6" squares for Corners:

Dark Blue	2	6" x 6"	H

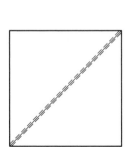
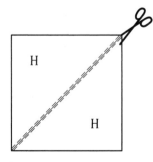

MAKE CORNERS H:

    Draw 1 diagonal line on each Corner square H.
    Sew a Stay-stitch ⅛" on each side of the diagonal line to stabilize the bias edge.
    Cut each square on the diagonal line.
    Label each piece H.

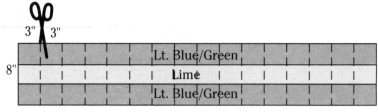

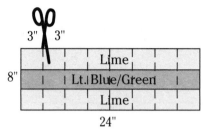

MAKE CHECKERBOARD SQUARES:

    Follow the instructions below for each color selection.

CHECKERBOARD A:

Checkerboard A - Rows 1 & 3:
    Sew 48" strips side by side to make a piece 8" x 48":
        Lime - Light Blue/Green - Lime.
    Cut 16 pieces 3" x 8".
    Label 8 pieces Row #1. Label 8 pieces Row #3.

Checkerboard A - Row 2:
    Sew 24" strips side by side to make a piece 8" x 24":
        Lime - Light Blue/Green - Lime.
    Cut 8 pieces 3" x 8" and label them Row #2.
    Sew the rows together. Press.
    Make 8 squares.
    Each Checkerboard will measure 8" x 8" at this point.

CHECKERBOARD B:

Checkerboard B - Rows 1 & 3:
    Sew 48" strips side by side to make a piece 8" x 48":
        Dark Blue/Green - Light Blue/Green - Dark Blue/Green.
    Make 2. Cut 32 pieces 3" x 8".
    Label 16 pieces Row #1. Label 16 pieces Row #3.

Checkerboard B - Row 2:
    Sew 48" strips side by side to make a piece 8" x 48":
        Light Blue/Green - Dark Blue/Green - Light Blue/Green.
    Cut 16 pieces 3" x 8" and label them Row #2.
    Sew the rows together. Press.
    Make 16 squares.
    Each Checkerboard will measure 8" x 8" at this point.

CHECKERBOARD C:

Checkerboard C - Rows 1 & 3:
    Sew 72" strips side by side to make a piece 8" x 72":
        Dark Blue/Green - Dark Blue - Dark Blue/Green.
    Make 2. Cut 48 pieces 3" x 8".
    Label 24 pieces Row #1. Label 24 pieces Row #3.

Checkerboard C - Row 2:
    Sew 72" strips side by side to make a piece 8" x 72":
        Dark Blue - Dark Blue/Green - Dark Blue.
    Cut 24 pieces 3" x 8" and label them Row #2.
    Sew the rows together. Press.
    Make 24 squares.
    Each Checkerboard will measure 8" x 8" at this point.

Keyhole - Rows Assembly Diagram

SEW EACH ROW TOGETHER:

Rows 1 & 17:
  Sew G - F - G. Press.

Rows 2 & 16:
  Sew G - F - F - F - G. Press.

Rows 3 & 15:
  Sew G - F - F - C - F - F - G. Press.

Rows 4 & 14:
  Sew G - F - F - C - G - C - F - F - G. Press.

Rows 5 & 13:
  Sew G - F - F - C - G - B - G - C - F - F - G. Press.

Rows 6 & 12:
  Sew G - F - F - C - G - B - E - B - G - C - F - F - G. Press.

Rows 7 & 11:
  Sew G - F - F - C - G - B - E - A - E - B - G - C - F - F - G. Press.

Row 8:
  Sew G - F - F - C - G - B - E - A - D - A - E - B - G - C - F - F. Press.

Row 9:
  Sew G - F - F - C - G - B - E - A - D - A - E - B - G - C - F - F - G. Press.

Row 10:
  Sew F - F - C - G - B - E - A - D - A - E - B - G - C - F - F - G. Press.

ASSEMBLY:
  Arrange all rows on a work surface or table.
  Refer to diagram for placement.
  Note: The rows are assembled from the lower left to the upper right.

  Sew rows together. Press.
  Corners - Sew a corner H to each corner. Press.

  Draw a line and trim so the outside edges are straight using a
  quilt ruler and the diagonals of the squares as a guide.

Outside Triangles

Dark Blue

Dark Blue-Green

Light Blue-Green

Lime

Lime

Lime

Light Blue-Green

Dark Blue-Green

Dark Blue

Outside Triangles

Keyhole - Quilt Assembly Diagram

FINISHING:
Quilting: See Basic Instructions.
Binding: Cut strips 2½" wide.
           Sew together end to end to equal 384".
           See Binding Instructions.

Big Blossoms

photo on pages 78 - 79

SIZE: 88" x 100"

YARDAGE:

We used Batik fabrics from *Hoffman*

Purchase the following Batik fabrics:

Blossoms	⅞ yard Blue
Blossoms	⅞ yard Brown
Blossoms	⅞ yard Green
Pieces F, G, J, & K	1¾ yards Tan
Row #1 & Checkerboards	1⅝ yards Golden Brown
Border #2, Checkerboards & Binding	1⅞ yards Dark Blue
Blossom Centers & Border #3	2⅔ yards Red
Backing	7⅔ yards
Batting	96" x 112"
Sewing machine, needle, thread	

CUTTING:

Label the pieces and stacks as you cut.

Color	Quantity	Size	Position
Blue	12	10" x 10"	Blossom 1, 5 & 9.
Brown	12	10" x 10"	Blossom 4, 7 & 8.
Green	12	10" x 10"	Blossom 2, 3 & 6.
Red	36	3" x 3"	Corners E
Tan	108	3" x 3"	Corners F
Tan	36	1½" x 7¼"	Lattice G
Red	18	1½" x 3¼"	Lattice H
Red	9	1½" x 6½"	Lattice I
Tan	18	1½" x 20½"	Block borders J
Tan	18	1½" x 22½"	Block borders K

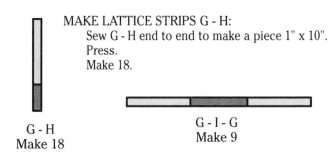

MAKE LATTICE STRIPS G - H:
  Sew G - H end to end to make a piece 1" x 10".
  Press.
  Make 18.

G - H
Make 18

G - I - G
Make 9

MAKE LATTICE STRIPS G - I - G:
  Sew G - I - G end to end to make a piece 1" x 20½".
  Press.
  Make 9.

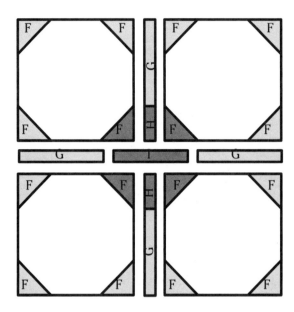

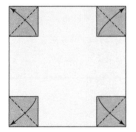 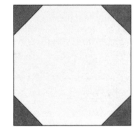

MAKE "SNOWBALL" SQUARES:
  Note: Make 12 squares with each color.
    Refer to the "Snowball" diagram.
    Align a Tan square F on 3 corners.
    Align a Red square E on the 4th corner.
    Draw a diagonal line from corner to corner
      on each small square.
  Sew on the line and fold back the triangle. Press.
  Repeat for all corners.
  Make 12 squares each of Blue, Brown & Green -
    36 squares total for 9 Blossoms.

ASSEMBLE BLOSSOM BLOCKS:
  Refer to the Block Assembly diagram.
Row 1: Sew 'Snowball' - Lattice G-H - 'Snowball'. Press.
Row 2: Use Lattice strip G-I-G.
Row 3: Sew 'Snowball' - Lattice G-H- 'Snowball'. Press.
    Sew the rows together. Press.

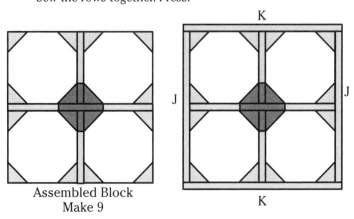

Assembled Block
Make 9

ADD BORDERS TO BLOSSOM BLOCKS:

  Sew a border J to the right and left sides of the block.
    Press.
  Sew a border K to the top and bottom of the block. Press.
  The block will measure 22½" x 22½" at this point.
  Make 9 blocks (3 blocks of each color).

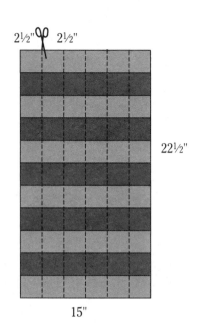

2½" ✂ 2½"

22½"

15"

MAKE CHECKERBOARD BORDERS:

Vertical Checkerboard Sashing - #1:
  Cut 6 Golden Brown strips 2½" x 15".
  Cut 5 Dark Blue strips 2½" x 15".
  Sew 11 Golden Brown and Dark Blue
    strips together side by side
    (alternating the colors)
    to make a piece 15" x 22½".
    Press.
  Cut the strip-set into 6 pieces,
    each 2½" x 22½".

Horizontal Checkerboard Sashing - #2:
  Cut 18 Golden Brown strips 2½" x 15".
  Cut 17 Dark Blue strips 2½" x 15".
  Sew 35 Golden Brown and Dark Blue
    strips together side by side
    (alternating the colors)
    to make a piece 15" x 70½".
    Press.
  Cut the strip-set into 6 pieces,
    each 2½" x 70½".

Side Checkerboard Borders - #3:
  Cut 22 Golden Brown strips 2½" x 5".
  Cut 23 Dark Blue strips 2½" x 5".
  Sew 45 Golden Brown and Dark Blue
    strips together side by side
    (alternating the colors)
    to make a piece 5" x 90½".
    Press.
  Cut the strip-set into 2 pieces,
    each 2½" x 90½".

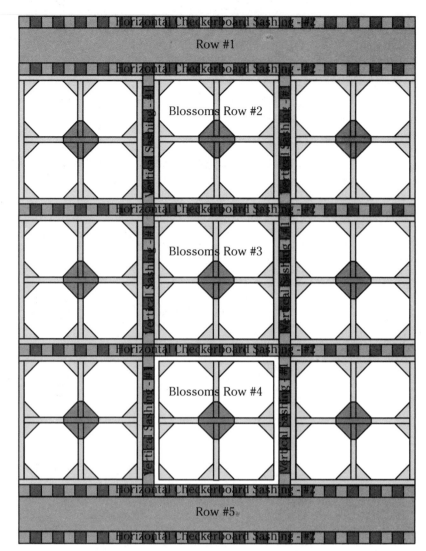

Big Blossoms - Quilt Assembly Diagram

PREPARE ROWS #1 & #5:
Rows #1 & #5:
  Cut 4 Golden Brown strips 6½" x width of fabric.
    Sew 2 strips together end to end for each row. Press.
  Cut 2 strips 6½" x 70½", one for each row.

PREPARE BLOSSOMS ROWS #2, #3 & #4:

Blossoms Row #2: Sew
  Blossom 1 - Sashing-1 - Blossom 2 - Sashing-1 - Blossom 3. Press.
Blossoms Row #3: Sew
  Blossom 4 - Sashing-1 - Blossom 5 - Sashing-1 - Blossom 6. Press.
Blossoms Row #4: Sew
  Blossom 7 - Sashing-1 - Blossom 8 - Sashing-1 - Blossom 9. Press.

QUILT ASSEMBLY:
Sew Rows Together:
  Sew the following:
  Sashing-2 - Row 1 - Sashing-2 - Row 2 - Sashing-2 - Row 3 - Sashing-2 -
    Row 4 - Sashing-2 - Row 5 - Sashing 2.
  Press.

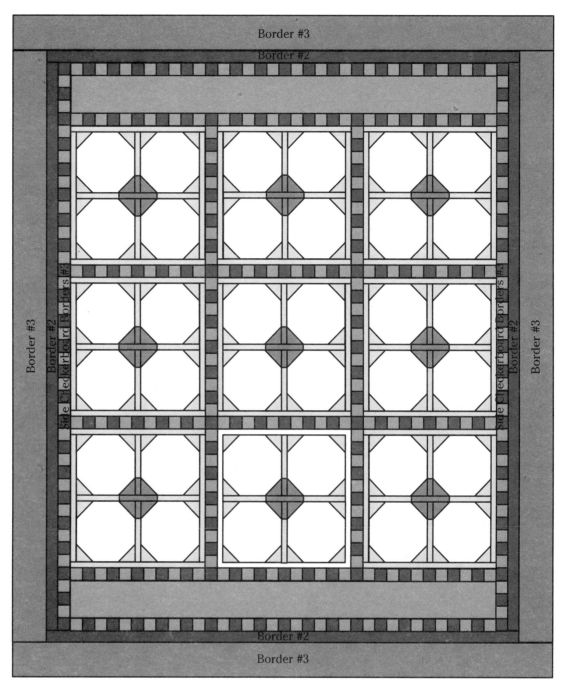

Big Blossoms - Borders Assembly Diagram

BORDERS:

Border #1:
    Sew a 2½" x 90½" Checkerboard strip to each
        side of the quilt. Press.

Border #2:
Cut 8 strips 1½" by the width of fabric.
Sew strips together end to end.
    Cut 2 strips 1½" x 90½" for sides.
    Cut 2 strips 1½" x 76½" for top and bottom.
    Sew side borders to the quilt. Press.
    Sew top and bottom borders to the quilt. Press.

Border #3:
Cut strips 6½" wide parallel to the selvage to
      eliminate piecing.
    Cut 2 strips 6½" x 92½" for sides.
    Cut 2 strips 6½" x 88½" for top and bottom.
    Sew side borders to the quilt. Press.
    Sew top and bottom borders to the quilt. Press.

FINISHING:
Quilting: See Basic Instructions.
Binding: Cut strips 2½" wide.
      Sew together end to end to equal 394".
      See Binding Instructions.

Butterflies in Bali

photo on pages 82 - 83

SIZE: 60" x 74"

YARDAGE:

We used Batik Fabric from *Hoffman*

Purchase the following Batik fabrics:

Butterfly bodies	⅛ yard Black
Butterfly #1 wings	⅙ yard Orange
Butterfly #2 Wings & Triangles	¾ yard Red
Butterfly #3 Wings & Border #4	⅝ yard Dark Red
Triangles	½ yard Gold
Butterfly background & Sashing	⅔ yard Cream
Cornerstones & Border #1	½ yard Dark Green
Border #3	⅜ yard Medium Green
Border #5 & Binding	1⅞ yards Brown-Green mix
Backing	3¾ yards
Batting	68" x 82"

Sewing machine, needle, thread
DMC Black pearl cotton or 6-ply floss
#22 or #24 chenille needle

Snowball Corner Diagram

"SNOWBALL" CORNERS:

Several strips in each block use the "Snowball" Corner technique. The direction of the diagonal for each strip in the block varies, so you must carefully note the diagonal on the block assembly diagram. Some strips have a "Snowball" corner on only one end. The squares used as "Snowball" Corners are labelled with a "c" in the cutting list.

Tip: Fold back the triangle and check its position before you sew.

Steps: Align a square with the appropriate end of the strip and sew on the diagonal line. Fold the triangle back and press before attaching it to any other strips.

CUTTING CHART FOR BUTTERFLIES
Cut all strips 2½" wide by the length specified.
Label the pieces by color as you cut.

SASHING STRIPS:

Color	Quantity	Length	Position
Cream	4	22½"	horizontal sashing
Cream	2	38½"	side sashing

BUTTERFLY #1:

Color	Quantity	Length	Position
Cream	1	10½"	21
	1	6½"	2
	6	4½"	10, 13, 14, 17, 19, 23
	6	2½"	1c, 3c, 15c, 15c, 16c, 16c
Orange	2	8½"	1, 3
	4	6½"	11, 12, 15, 16
	2	4½"	4, 9
	10	2½"	2c, 2c, 6, 7, 10c, 13c, 20, 21c, 21c, 22
Black	1	6½"	18
Red	2	4½"	5, 8
Dark Red	2	2½"	11c, 12c

BUTTERFLY #2:

Color	Quantity	Length	Position
Cream	1	10½"	21
	1	6½"	2
	6	4½"	10, 13, 14, 17, 19, 23
	6	2½"	1c, 3c, 15c, 15c, 16c, 16c
Red	2	8½"	1, 3
	4	6½"	11, 12, 15, 16
	2	4½"	4, 9
	10	2½"	2c, 2c, 6, 7, 10c, 13c, 20, 21c, 21c, 22
Black	1	6½"	18
Dark Red	2	4½"	5, 8
	2	2½"	11c, 12c

BUTTERFLY #3:

Color	Quantity	Length	Position
Cream	1	10½"	21
	1	6½"	2
	6	4½"	10, 13, 14, 17, 19, 23
	6	2½"	1c, 3c, 15c, 15c, 16c, 16c
Dark Red	2	8½"	1, 3
	4	6½"	11, 12, 15, 16
	2	4½"	4, 9
	10	2½"	2c, 2c, 6, 7, 10c, 13c, 20, 21c, 21c, 22
Black	1	6½"	18
Red	2	4½"	5, 8
	2	2½"	11c, 12c

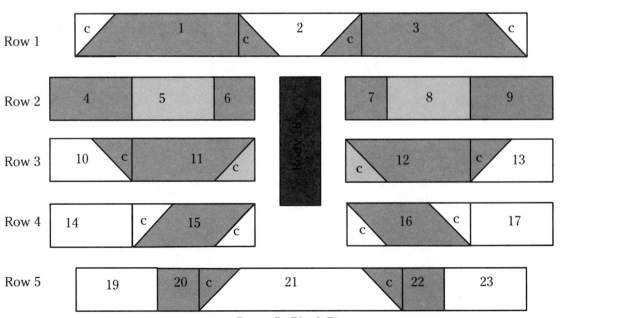

Butterfly Block Diagram

SEW CORNERS TO STRIPS:

Refer to the "Snowball" Corners diagram.
You need the following "c" squares:
1c, both 2c's, 3c, 10c, 11c, 12c, 13c, both 15c's, both 16c's, and both 21c's.
Align a square on each strip as shown in the diagram.
Carefully note the direction of each diagonal.
Draw the diagonal lines and sew on the line.
Fold back the flaps and press.

Row 1: Sew 1 "Snowball" corner to strips 1 & 3.
Sew 2 "Snowball" corners to strip 2.
Row 3: Sew 1 "Snowball" corner to strips 10, 11, 12 & 13.
Row 4: Sew 2 "Snowball" corners to strips 15 & 16.
Row 5: Sew 2 "Snowball" corners to strip 21.

SEW BUTTERFLY ROWS TOGETHER:

Row 1: Sew 1-2-3 together. Press.
Row 2: Sew 4-5-6 together. Press. Sew 7-8-9 together. Press.
Row 3: Sew 10-11 together. Press. Sew 12-13 together. Press.
Row 4: Sew 14-15 together. Press. Sew 16-17 together. Press.
Row 5: Sew 19-20-21-22-23 together. Press.

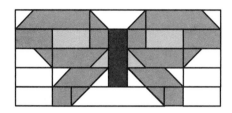

BUTTERFLY ASSEMBLY FOR CENTER:

Sew the following pieces in a column:
Left Side - Sew 4-5-6 to 10-11 to 14-15. Press.
Right Side - Sew 7-8-9 to 12-13 to 16-17. Press.
Assemble the Body -
Sew the Left side - Body 18 - Right side. Press.
Sew Rows 1 - 2/3/4 - 5. Press.

Each block will measure 10½" x 22½" at this point.
Make 3 butterfly blocks.

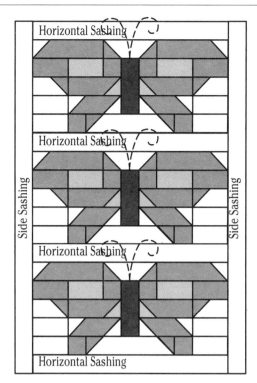

Butterflies in Bali - Butterflies Assembly Diagram

ASSEMBLY:

Arrange all blocks on a work surface or table.
Refer to the Assembly diagram for placement.
Sew the following together:
Horizontal Sashing - Butterfly 1 -
Horizontal Sashing - Butterfly 2 -
Horizontal Sashing - Butterfly 3 -
Horizontal Sashing. Press.
Sew the following together:
Side Sashing - Butterfly unit - Side Sashing.
Press.

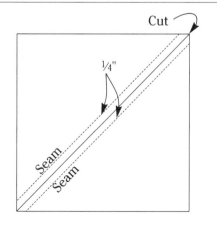

Half-Square Triangle Diagram
1. Place 2 squares right sides together.
2. Draw a diagonal line from corner to corner.
3. Stitch ¼" on each side of the line.
4. Cut squares apart on the diagonal line.
5. Open the 2 new squares with 2 colors.
6. Press. Trim off dog-ears.
7. Center and trim to size.

PREPARE BLOCKS FOR BORDER #2:

Label the blocks as you make them.

Block A - Half-square triangles for Borders:
Cut 10 Red squares 7½" x 7½".
Cut 10 Gold squares 7½" x 7½".
Pair up 10 units of Red - Gold squares.
Follow the instructions in the Half-Square Triangle Diagram to make 20 half-square triangles.
Trim each square to 6½" x 6½".
Label each square "A".

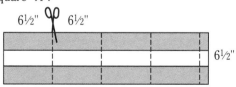

Block B - for Sides:
Cut 2 Red strips 2½" x 27".
Cut 1 Dark Green strip 2½" x 27".
Sew a Red - Dark Green - Red together side by side to make a piece 6½" x 27". Press.
Cut strip-set into 4 pieces 6½" x 6½".

Block C - for Corners:
Cut 4 Dark Green squares 6½" x 6½" for Corners.

Pieced Top Border #2

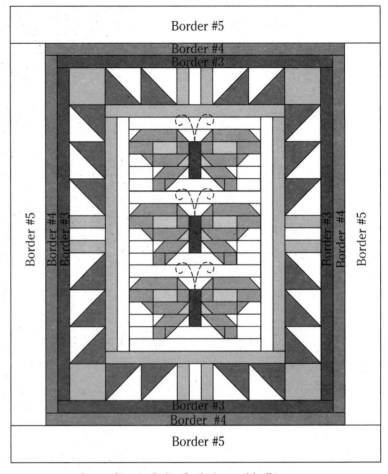

Butterflies in Bali - Center Assembly Diagram

Butterflies in Bali - Quilt Assembly Diagram

PIECED BORDERS:

Border #1:

Cut 2 strips 2½" x 38½" for sides.
Cut 2 strips 2½" x 30½" for top and bottom.
Sew side borders to the quilt. Press.
Sew top and bottom borders to the quilt. Press.

Pieced Border #2:

Refer to the Quilt Assembly diagram for placement.

Side Borders - #2:
Sew A-A-A-B-A-A-A. Press. Make 2.
Sew side borders to the quilt. Press.

Top & Bottom Borders - #2:
Sew C-A-A-B-A-A-C. Press. Make 2.
Sew top and bottom borders to the quilt. Press.

ADDITIONAL BORDERS:

Border #3:

Cut 5 strips 2½" by the width of fabric.
Sew the strips together end to end.

Cut 2 strips 2½" x 54½" for sides.
Cut 2 strips 2½" x 44½" for top and bottom.
Sew side borders to the quilt. Press.
Sew top and bottom borders to the quilt. Press.

Border #4:

Cut 6 strips 2½" by the width of fabric.
Sew strips together end to end.

Cut 2 strips 2½" x 58½" for sides.
Cut 2 strips 2½" x 48½" for top and bottom.
Sew side borders to the quilt. Press.
Sew top and bottom borders to the quilt. Press.

Border #5:

Cut strips 6½" wide parallel to the selvage to
eliminate piecing.

Cut 2 strips 6½" x 62½" for sides.
Cut 2 strips 6½" x 60½" for top and bottom.
Sew side borders to the quilt. Press.
Sew top and bottom borders to the quilt. Press.

FINISHING:

Embroidery:

Mark antennae on the quilt with a
disappearing pen.
Sew a long and short Running stitch to
make the antennae.

Quilting: See Basic Instructions.

Binding: Cut strips 2½" wide.
Sew together end to end to equal 278".
See Binding Instructions

Color Wheel in Blue

pieced by Rose Ann Pegram
quilted by Susan Corbett

Inspired by the spinning colors in a kite at a country market, this quilt radiates exciting colors, fabulous quilting and fun movement.

instructions on pages 19 - 21

Spinning colors

Colorful Ikat fabrics

Woven Songket fabrics

Beautiful Batiks

Woven with Silver

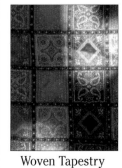

Woven Tapestry

Tradition is carefully followed.

Using a small mirror

Applying make up

Each flower is separate.

Typical costume

pieced by Lanelle Herron
quilted by Julie Lawson

Arts flourish, a true tradition of craftsmanship carries importance in many places and villages of skilled artisans survive in Bali.

Cottage industry, in particular handicrafts, has allowed local economies to shift away from agriculture while maintaining a rural culture.

Dancing Ladies

Dancers clothed in symbolic make up and costumes perform cultural stories of the relationship between good and evil.

see instructions on pages 48 - 49

Typical dancer

Young dancers

Dramatic stories

Dancers begin as children.

Discussing the dance

Gracious, welcoming, charming – the old fashioned, magical gardens of former Miss Texas Mary Nell (Hendricks) Hubbard bring beauty to her home.

A lifelong lover of flowers and wildlife, Mary Nell was inspired to create her garden when she needed subjects for her beautiful watercolor paintings. She is a Master Gardener and has designed a lovely organically maintained garden that has grown into a lush oasis.

Peaceful water features, visual movement, garden art, line and color make it a perfect backdrop in which to showcase the beautiful Batik quilts.

Doing tricks on an elephant

Ada is a professional artist.

Picking out colors

Painting with a tiny brush

Elephant Walk

pieced by Kayleen Allen
quilted by Susan Corbett

Small Batik panels of elephants are the core of this simple quilt. I sketched the elephants, then they were done in traditional Batik while I was in Bali. They remind me of this special day with an elephant. Other Batik panels and subjects would work equally well.

Relationships between elephants and people can last a lifetime. "Ada" has learned to paint with a small brush and her large trunk. Watching her is quite amazing. This quilt was inspired by her choice of colors.

see instructions on pages 50 - 51

Riding an Elephant

BATIKS... Inspired by Bali 71

Friendly and shy

Waiting in her shop

Preparing offering baskets

Brushing his teeth

Hand weaving expert

Village Square

pieced by Rose Ann Pegram
quilted by Sue Needle

My journey into the beautiful highlands and traditional villages inspired this colorful quilt. Villages are essentially a religious community organized around a series of temples, a market and civic structures.

The majority of traditional rural people live in tight village communities with large extended families. Home compounds are usually laid out on a north-south orientation and may include several families and generations. Usually village land is considered to be a legacy of the founding ancestors.

see instructions on pages 52 - 53

Baskets for roosters

Protection from the sun

Cooking in a kitchen

Carrying supplies

The wood carver

Heading for home

Shopping in town

Preparation for supper

Crossing paths

Everyday chores

Baskets and Sarongs

pieced by Lanelle Herron
quilted by Julie Lawson

Traditional Balinese dress calls for a sarong wrap and a waist sash. Both men and women may wear comfortable and colorful sarongs in everyday dress.

As close to beauty, and as far from ordinary as you can get. Most people live in rural villages and rely on traditional foot transportation in the fields. With a culture that thrives on traditional values and magnificent vistas, Bali is an unspoiled and unbelievably beautiful land.

see instructions on pages 54 - 57

Traditional Batik sarong

Carrying mattresses

Mother and children

Modern and ancient

Keeping out of the sun

A home in the country

An active volcano in the distance

Surrounded by rice

Important terraces for rice

Homeward bound

Keyhole

pieced by Kayleen Allen
quilted by Sue Needle

Experience the beautiful colors of nature. Fields of green rice, water and blue sky make the world go around. Bali's rice terraces are among some of the most famed and spectacular in the world. Every time I look at this colorful coverlet I explore the timelessness of the countryside.

Keyholes and gateways represent the dividing line between the inner and outer worlds. Door panels and window shutters are highly adorned with the object of protecting the building from evil "intruders".

see instructions on pages 58 - 60

Ornate door carvings

Doorway in the palace

Stairs keep homes safe

Carved front doors

Working in the courtyard

Dressed for a festival

Yummy ice cream

Playing with a kite

Best friends

Ceremonial music

Cooling off mid-day

Big Blossoms

pieced by Donna Perrotta
quilted by Julie Lawson

The growth of flowers signifies beauty and rebirth. Lush vegetation is both relaxing and refreshing. Curling up on a garden bench with a good book and wrapped in a warm quilt is a great way to begin any day.

Blossoms and flowers are symbols of beauty. In Bali small blossoms are gathered fresh as they drop from trees. Every day they are placed in offerings to spirits in temples and homes.

see instructions on pages 61 - 63

Carved stone in the garden

Statues from volcanic stone

Symbolic goddess

The royal waterpark

Carved stone sculpture

Roots of a sacred tree

Light Blues

Dark Blues

Dark Greens

Lime & Tans

Purples

Golds & Ivory

Blacks

Reds

Batik Fabrics

'Bali Pops' are 2¹/₂" strips of Batik fabrics, available in color-coordinated and pre-cut packs.

'Fat Quarters' are 18" x 22" fabric pieces, often available in collections.

Your private stash of assorted fabrics is a perfect source for quilts.

All of these designs can be made from or supplemented with yardage.

Cut fabric into pieces with a rotary cutter, quilter's ruler and cutting mat.

Sorting Batik 'Bali Pop' Fabrics

Sorting Batik fabrics into stacks of similar colors is an important step. It is fun and can be challenging at the same time.

Begin by sorting strips by color. All instructions for the 'Bali Pop' quilts in this book begin with a sorting technique – such as all "Dark Blues" are listed under one color category for strips. This may take a little creative thinking since the "Dark Blue" stack may contain Darks of Blue, Purple, Dark Purple and various related prints.

You are finished sorting when every color stack has the indicated quantity of strips. You may need to be more creative to shift strips back and forth until all colors seem to "fit" somewhere. And while you are sewing, remember to be creative and flexible. A lot of the beauty of Batiks is the subtle and unexpected color shifts.

The photo above shows how colors can be grouped and labeled.

Once all the colors are sorted, you are ready to begin sewing.

Note: Of course if you purchase Batik' yardage instead of using a 'Bali Pop', all the "Dark Blues" will be one color, so sorting is simple.

SUPPLIERS

Most quilt and fabric stores carry an excellent assortment of supplies. If you need something special, ask your local store to contact the following companies.

BATIK FABRICS and 'BALI POPS'-
Hoffman California Fabrics,
Mission Viejo, CA 92691

'CIRCLE' & 'DIAMOND' TEMPLATES -
June Taylor
Richfield, WI 53076

'FAT CATS' TEMPLATE -
Wm. Wright
Antioch, TN 37013

QUILTING BY
Susan Corbett, 817-361-7762
Julie Lawson, 817-428-5929
Sue Needle, 817-589-1168

WANT TO TRAVEL?

When you get itchy feet to travel, consider contacting one of the following companies. I have not traveled with all of them and they may not go to Bali, but I'm sure they specialize in adventures and visit exotic places. I have heard good reports from friends.

JOURNEY ENCOUNTER
M. Douglas Walton
Ruston, LA   318-247-8707
mdouglaswalton.com

CRAFT WORLD TOURS (CWT) -
Tom Muir Wilson
Byron, N.Y.   585-548-2667
craftworldtours.com

SEW MANY PLACES
Jim West
Spring Valley, IL   1-877-887-1188
sewmanyplaces.com

McCALL'S QUILTING -
Steve
Golden, CO   1-877-64-QUILT
steve@McCallsQuiltingAdventures.com

MANY THANKS to my staff for their cheerful help and wonderful ideas!

Kathy Mason • Patty Williams
Donna Kinsey • Janet Long
David & Donna Thomason